THE
CULTURE
WARRIOR

Leadership Lessons from Joe Scarlett

Copyright © 2023 Joe Scarlett
All rights reserved
First Edition

PAGE PUBLISHING
Conneaut Lake, PA

First originally published by Page Publishing 2023

ISBN 979-8-88793-921-6 (pbk)
ISBN 979-8-88793-948-3 (hc)
ISBN 979-8-88793-941-4 (digital)

Printed in the United States of America

I've studied, written about, and worked with great business leaders for over 40 years. If I were asked to suggest one resource on leadership, it would be Joe Scarlett's new book, The Culture Warrior. What differentiates Joe as a leader is not just his extraordinary track record of success, but his wisdom. Joe's insights are a blueprint for leadership grounded in vision, values, and creating a culture that gets the job done. I give The Culture Warrior my absolute highest recommendation.

Joe Calloway—Author—Becoming A Category Of One

I am very grateful Joe Scarlett has placed his leadership wisdom in one place for generations of leaders to read. For many years, I have benefited from Joe's example of leadership characterized by excellence, compassion and integrity, his patient and impactful mentoring, and his insightful speaking and writing. This is a book I will enthusiastically recommend to every emerging and experienced leader I know.

Art Athens
Retired Marine Corps Colonel
Former Director, U.S. Naval Academy Stockdale
Center for Ethical Leadership
U.S. Naval Academy's First Distinguished
Military Professor of Leadership

I've had the good fortune of knowing Joe Scarlett for over twenty years and have benefited significantly from his knowledge and wisdom. There are very few people in this world who've enjoyed his level of business success. His willingness to share his leadership principles is a blessing for us all. Sound business and leadership practices that actually work! Thanks Joe!!

Mark Emkes
Retired Chairman, CEO, and President of Bridgestone
Americas Former Commissioner of Finance and
Administration, State of Tennessee

"Wisdom is supreme; therefore get wisdom." This was King Solomon's advice to young people back in his day, per Proverbs 4 of the NIV Bible. That truth and advice is just as important in today's world for those who aspire to be successful leaders. Joe Scarlett provides insights in this book that can be so valuable to those who seek to "get wisdom." He has it, he's demonstrated it, and he's sharing it.

Tom Moser—Retired vice chairman of KPMG, who has served as a director for various business and charitable organizations

There are great leaders and then there are great leaders who develop other great leaders. Joe Scarlett is the latter. As a former supplier to Tractor Supply Company, I always looked forward to hearing his talks on leadership and organizational development at the various events he spoke at. In retirement he has continued to share his wisdom through teaching and through the articles he has written. I am so thankful he has compiled all of his wisdom and insights into a book. It's a must read, and a resource you will want to keep close for years to come.

Randy Boyd, President of the University of Tennessee

The success that Joe Scarlett has experienced in his professional career in retail is unparalleled. In this masterful compilation of his numerous articles on leadership and culture, he shares his sage insights and formulas for success. This work contains pragmatic "golden nuggets" in every chapter, and is an easy and helpful read for business owners and managers at virtually any stage of their career. This book should be on the required reading list for all University business students.

Paul C. Stumb, Ph.D. President
Cumberland University

In "Culture Warrior," Joe Scarlett, a revered former Fortune 500 executive, shares profound articles that reveal the secrets of effective leadership and success. With engaging storytelling and real-world examples, Scarlett unveils the vital connection between culture and leadership. Gain actionable knowledge on fostering empowering cultures, effective communication, trust-building, and purpose-driven leadership. "Culture Warrior" is a treasure trove of practical wisdom, empowering you to unlock your leadership potential and achieve organizational greatness.

Mila Grigg, CEO MODA Image & Brand Consulting
and author of #1 Best-seller of FORGED BY FIRE

INTRODUCTION

I consider myself a Culture Warrior—but not in the way you might expect. I am passionate about building a business culture that sustains and encourages growth and success. With enough money, one can easily replicate the assets of a competitor; but replicating the culture is a much larger challenge and, in many cases, proves impossible. A strong, well-conceived company culture is the competitive edge that can propel your organization to the top of the hill.

Leadership dictates the culture—or, in some cases, the lack of culture—in any organization. Great leaders realize that culture is the most important component in the success of most every business: build a good one and the sky is the limit. Tolerate a bad culture, and the future will likely be grim. Leaders build strong cultures by setting the right example for their team. Effective leaders set the culture by regularly talking about the mission, the values, and a shared vision for the future.

My own understanding of the importance of culture did not develop overnight. It came about through years of on-the-job observation, experience and listening. Perhaps the strongest voice in this area was that of Tom Hennesy my former mentor and business partner who preached that the number one motivator is recognition. By taking that thought and running with it, he turned our company into a strongly recognition-focused organization. Through this, I learned that celebrating success, no matter how big or small, begets success—the scale of which could be even bigger the next time around. I know now that culture starts with leadership.

From the time I was a youngster, I absorbed lessons in leadership from my father who regularly associated with business executives from a variety of industries. He shared his observations about character, style, and strategy, plus a whole lot more. We talked and I learned. Sparked by these early father-son conversations, leadership has evolved into a personal passion of mine.

In my first real job, I held a series of leadership positions for a discount store chain over a fifteen-year period. Several good mentors along the way taught me a lot about leadership and management. Perhaps even more importantly, I learned a lot about what not to do. As I like to say: if you get your nose bloodied once, you won't go down that path again.

Opportunity brought me to Tractor Supply Company, where I spent nearly thirty years and advanced from Vice President to CEO. A group of us bought the company and twelve years later, took it public. We started with 100 stores. Today, there are more than 2,000. Study the numbers and you will find that Tractor Supply Company is one of the best long-term performers in the S&P 500. I firmly believe this success can be credited in large part to a very positive business culture, one envied by competitors and peers alike.

As a student of leadership for more than half a century, I have watched, observed, studied, associated with, and read about great leaders. I have also worked to share much of what I have learned with others. As my retirement from Tractor Supply approached, I took over a local leadership program and ultimately ran it for eight years. I began my tenure with that program by asking the CEOs of 35 companies the following question: what skills do your upwardly mobile executives need to launch them to the next level? Across the board, answers involved the "soft skills"—team building, coaching, counseling, public speaking—the same skills that I see as integral to developing leaders who will carry out a strong and healthy corporate culture. It is my opinion that folks like me have an obligation to give the up-and-comers all the counseling and advice we can provide.

This book is comprised of 150 articles written between 2008 and 2022. Most were published in the Nashville Business Journal, with several appearing in other newspapers. You will find more than two dozen articles related to my favorite topic: management and leadership skills. As you will see, I also touch on the importance of ethical behavior in and out of the business world. These articles are separated into twelve topic-driven chapters, with the addition of one chapter containing miscellaneous op-eds. It is my sincere hope that reading these articles will help you improve your leadership skills at least in some small way.

A big "Thank You" to my niece, Julie Kailus, who for fifteen years kept me out of trouble by editing my articles. Plus, a special "Thank You" to my wife Dorothy, my most trusted advisor, and to Katie Hazelwood, my newest partner in writing.

Comments and suggestions are welcome at joe@joescarlett.com.

CONTENTS

1. Career 1
2. Skills 25
3. Character 65
4. Communication 83
5. Leadership 98
6. Ethics 128
7. Decisions 145
8. Culture 153
9. Talent 171
10. Strategy 189
11. Teamwork 204
12. Family 212
13. Scarlett op-eds 221

1. CAREER

Build your skills
NBJ April 18, 2014 (Orig. Take charge of your career)

If you let random events develop your career it might be just that—an unsteady path. Or you can be proactive, taking charge of the direction of your work and life. Assuming you select the second option, here are a few thoughts to put you on the best possible track.

The first challenge is to figure out where you want your career to go. You may already have a plan but you can benefit further from talking to other guides. Start by discussing your career intentions with your boss to see what the future might hold. Then consider seeking out other leaders within your business and HR department. Ask the advice of a mentor if you have one. I found that talking to my father, who was also a businessman, helped me to focus my career.

Once you a have a clear idea of where you want to go, it's time to map out a specific plan to move in the right direction. Set up a personal advancement agenda. Keep in mind that a career-development plan is not short term—it will span several years. Start by asking yourself these questions:

- ➤ What books, magazines, trade journals, etc. do I need to be reading?
- ➤ What business experiences should I try to get on my agenda and make a priority?
- ➤ Should I request a transfer to a different role to learn new skills?

> What developmental classes could I take to further my proficiencies?
> Who should be on my list of networking targets and how much time can I dedicate to networking each week?

The goal is to craft a plan that gives you the exposure, experiences and knowledge to move ahead. You may have to push others to get it all done, but some assertiveness may reflect well on your ambition to get ahead. However, as you seek counsel and develop a plan of action, be sure to keep your family in the loop. For example, if you are pursuing a career goal that will result in moving to another city, it's critical that your family is engaged and supportive.

Take charge of your career—don't leave it to chance. Build a plan, stick to it, modify goals as necessary and don't give up. Your diligence will pay off. As one business sage I know has always said, "You will get that promotion long after you think you should have gotten it—and when you least expect it." So be prepared.

Get busy and take charge of your career
NBJ January 27, 2017

You can either let circumstances set your career path or you can take charge. You may not achieve everything you desire but you can certainly shape much of your future by the actions you take. Your career will last a long time so be patient, persistent and committed to where you want to go.

Making a career choice: If you are already set on a career path that you're passionate about, great. If not get going now by looking at every possibility that you think might be right for you and your skill set. Some of those old career-guidance tests from high school might be of help. You can also ask friends what they like and don't like about their jobs; study occupation openings online and in the paper; learn about current compensation for different positions; and seek out possible career mentors. You may not yet zero in on a clear choice but you will narrow the possibilities.

Building your skills: Find out what skills will be necessary for your No. 1 career choice and build a plan to obtain those faculties. Gather all your contacts—managers, peers, HR department, friends—who could guide you in skill development. And, when necessary, get creative. At one point in my career, I was given supervisory responsibility over the IT department but knew little or nothing about the operations. I immediately signed up for a one-week IBM course appropriately titled "Supervisory skills for those without technical background," which gave me some quick-and-dirty basic skills for my new responsibility. Be proactive. Do whatever it takes to build your skill base.

Studying core companies: You can't necessarily choose your employer but you can narrow the field. Build a target list and focus on that list. Start by studying the reputations of those core companies, and then network with industry players who can help you gain greater insight. If you have a high-risk mindset, you could widen your scope by seeking out non-traditional employers or corporate setups that might lead to some unusual or more challenging opportunities.

Finding the right job: The best way to approach your job search is to remember this: Full-time jobs require your attention for at least 40 hours a week—and so does the job of finding a job. Build a good resume and get some outside help to make sure you're putting your best foot forward. Then go to work—send resumes, call key people, knock on doors, dress the part, be polite in every interaction, even charm receptionists if you have to. Use every arrow in your quiver. Bottom line: Be persistent. Most employers will admire your perseverance.

Whether you are just starting out or have been in business for years, there's no time like the present to take charge of your career. Your initiative, conduct and tenacity will be rewarded.

Building blocks to jump-start your career
NBJ Feb 2011; (Orig. Personal Preparation)

A wise friend once said, "You will get that promotion long after you think you should have gotten it and when you least expect it."

In business, all we can do is to be as prepared as possible for what may come our way. Preparation is fundamental to career success. No matter where you are today, always be preparing yourself for the next step in your career. Even if you don't exactly know what that step is, do everything in your power to get ready. Here's how:

Build a personal niche: Businesses are continually searching for that differentiated niche in the market that will yield competitive advantage. You can follow that same path by carving out a niche for yourself. Become an authority on a topic in your organization. Become so knowledgeable that you are considered the "go-to person" on a least one subject. Go-to people are both respected and admired.

Volunteer: Volunteer for special assignments, particularly on new projects or when the challenges will be the toughest. Embrace change and be a positive champion of it in your organization. Being open to change and volunteering gives you new and different experiences and often opens the door for career growth. And when times are tough, your boss will not forget those who helped and embraced change.

Live like a leader: As a professional and a leader, everything you do and say is likely being observed. You are always "on stage." One of my mentors coached me to dress for the job you want, not the one you have. Start by benchmarking your personal appearance against the most respected leaders in your organization. And remember to smile, be a good conversationalist and consistently act like the consummate professional, because you never know who's watching.

Recognize performance: Be a positive influence on others. Sincere recognition is the number one motivator, so don't be shy about congratulating others with a simple pat on the back or a nice note. You don't have to be the boss to hand out accolades; often a positive word from a peer can mean as a much or more than the same words from a boss. Try it. You will feel good, and those you recognize will develop a new-found respect for you.

Associate with winners: Get to know the "movers and the shakers," particularly those in more senior roles in your organization. Also, start to associate with your competitive peers inside and outside your company. Participate in professional groups and trade organizations to broaden your contacts and your knowledge. Make a point to have lunch with a different person every day. Making winning associations can advance your career in more ways than you can count.

Become a communications pro: Effective writing is a basic building block of success—and practice is the key to improvement. If your writing skills could use some polishing, find a friend who can critique and coach your writing. Also, practice your conversational skills and be prepared to ask good questions and then listen—very carefully—to what others are saying. And as scary as it may be, speak in front of groups at every opportunity. Public speaking also gets better with practice. You can influence your career more through effective communications skills than in any other way.

Make your career move—stay flexible, prepared, involved
NBJ October 22, 2010

Finding a real career is about finding our way. Few of us begin a business career with a clear, long-term direction. Rather, most of us spend a few years learning and adjusting before settling on a general direction. And those plans are *still* subject to change.

In fact, remaining flexible may be a boon for your career. You may wind up in a position far different than you originally intended—and happier in it. As a good friend of the Scarlett Leadership Institute always says, "You will receive that big promotion way after you think you should have received it and when you least expect it."

As we experiment, fine-tune our skill set and learn how to function and achieve within an organization, our knowledge and confidence grows and we mature in the professional world. Along the way we might also earn one or two low-level promotions. It is also likely that we screw up several times and get our nose properly bloodied. That's how we learn.

But while we all need sufficient time to find our way in the professional world, there are a few tips that can help you do that a little quicker—and with fewer bloody noses.

Prepare: Being prepared in every possible way is one of the keys to building your career. Study all that you can; subscribe to trade journals; dig deeper on the Web; go to seminars; and learn from your colleagues. You can set yourself apart by becoming an expert in some aspect of your business. Work at becoming the "go-to person" on one topic. When you earn go-to status on a subject, you are automatically more valuable to your company and you gain the respect of others in the organization.

Get involved: Keep up with the developments in your organization: new products, special initiatives, process changes, expansion, etc. Change in an organization often creates opportunities, and you want to be ready to take advantage of those when they arise. Volunteer for special projects. You will learn new things, possibly meet key executives and will likely be recognized for your contribution. Seek out those special assignments—in many cases they lead to big career opportunities.

Network: Networking inside and outside your company is another important aspect of building your career. The better connected you are, the greater access you have to information, which can set you apart from the pack and help you gain recognition in your industry. Take every opportunity to associate with both peers and superiors in your organization. Attend professional events; make an effort to meet as many key people as you can; collect business cards and stay in touch; and don't waste your lunch break eating at your desk—it's a great time to network.

Act the part: At the Scarlett Leadership Institute, we often use the phrase "leaders are always on stage," which means that everything we do and say is being observed in some way by others. It is important to our long-term growth to maintain a professional approach in everything we do and with every person we meet.

Stay cool and professional under all circumstances—it will pay off in the long run. Your personal appearance and conduct are also extremely important, so dress for the job you want, shake hands with confidence and always wear a smile.

Employers seek individuals with knowledge, energy, enthusiasm, ambition and a positive attitude. If you strive for these core values, your career may just fall in your lap.

Quit job-hopping: stick with a quality employer
NBJ May 20, 2016. (Orig. Stick with a quality employer)

Did you know 21% of workers plan to leave their job in 2016? That's up from 16% last year. Run the numbers and you'll see that this translates to slightly less than five average years on the job! That means workers could have up to 10 employers during a lifetime.

Times have certainly changed our concept of career. Other than part-time and temporary jobs in my youth, I have worked for only two companies. By today's standards I'm a dinosaur. But maybe there's something you can learn from my Jurassic approach.

My first employer was a discount store chain in New Jersey. This high-growth company provided plenty of opportunity for a young buck like me. However, there were some dark clouds on the horizon that made me realize that the future was grim. My next step was to join Tractor Supply, where I stayed for nearly three decades.

Seeing opportunity through turmoil: There are certainly solid reasons to change employers to protect your career, such as a company that's clearly heading to a dead-end, taking you with it. However, there is also big opportunity in businesses that are going through tough times, which was the case when I first joined Tractor Supply. Out of the operational mess during my first two years emerged a reorganization that put the company on a 35-year course of continuous growth and improvement. I did not jump ship during the early years because I could see a future for the business.

When you think about moving on to another employer take a good look at your current situation first. You have likely already invested years, learned the culture, built a reputation and honed your skills at this company. Ask yourself:

1. What are my opportunities with my current employer?
2. Can I discuss the future with my boss and/or human resource department?
3. Can I carve out a new position that will best leverage my skill set to take the company forward?
4. Do I really want to abandon my professional investment and start over?
5. Will moving to another company mean I won't run into the same professional challenges?

If you can step back and see the bigger picture, perhaps you'll find that the best long-term opportunity for your career is staying right where you are. After all, management teams know that promoting from within an organization typically yields substantially better results than the new hire. In fact, research shows that CEOs promoted from within an organization have twice the success rate as CEOs hired from outside. Plus switching employers requires starting at the bottom, and relearning an entirely new culture and professional hierarchy.

It may sound old-fashioned, but the most successful people I know have committed to a career at a few superior companies rather than perpetual job-hopping. Considering your long-term stability and financial growth, the best odds may be finding—and sticking with—a quality employer.

Management career stuck in neutral? Learn to delegate
2009

Have you ever worked for a leader you would describe as a **"micro manager"?** Not very satisfying, and not much fun, was it?

THE CULTURE WARRIOR

Career growth is often stalled by an inability and an unwillingness to effectively delegate responsibility. Managers who are reluctant to trust and empower others may find themselves unable to move ahead in an organization.

When we were young and first entered the work force, we were given a task to do and, because we did such a good job, we were soon given more tasks. Over time we became more proficient at completing the tasks and were promoted to a managerial position with several employees reporting to us. Then, we worked even more hours to demonstrate our dedication to the job. As a boss, we knew best how to do everything, so there was little reason to spend a lot of time with our employees training them to do work we were so good at.

And so, we worked our way up the ladder doing much of the detail work ourselves. We gave orders to our employees and then looked over their shoulders to make sure the work was done just like we would do it. We became expert "micro-managers" and as a result, probably stalled our career growth.

Hold everything! If you have the word "manager" in your title you are supposed to lead others on your Team. You are not supposed to do all the work yourself. Managing is traditionally defined as "getting work done through others." Think about that.

Early in my managerial career, I had the responsibility for about a dozen people to accomplish a specific project, and when I thought I had everything covered, I started doing a task myself. A savvy senior manager pulled me aside and showed me that a third of my team was not actually working. Lo and behold, I was unaware because I was too busy on my own manual tasks!

He encouraged me to think of myself as an orchestra conductor who must get a group of musicians who play different instruments to produce beautiful music. In managerial terms, that translates to getting a group of individuals to complete the various tasks that together accomplish the job at hand. This transformational lesson put me on a path to become a trusting and empowering delegator.

Your ability to effectively delegate is essential to your career growth—define, assign, follow-up, evaluate, and give credit for achievement. Your role as a leader is simply to get the job done. Don't confuse activity (like working a lot of hours) with accomplishment (achieving the goal.) Your bottom-line responsibility as a manager is accomplishing the mission at hand.

Trust is the key component in effective delegation. You've got to be able to trust your people. Stressed-out because you don't have your hand in everything? Get over it! Get the right people on the Team and give them clear direction. You can't do it all yourself—get used to trusting others. An empowered, high-quality team with a clear mission is your ticket to success.

Leaders keep their head up because they are not immersed in the details. Leaders have the time to see "over the hill" and "around the corner". No matter what your leadership position is today, the ability to delegate effectively is one of the key components to successful career growth over the long term.

Career evolution: you can change your behavior
NBJ June 10, 2016

As you grow in your career, the nature of your role and responsibilities requires changes in behavior. What's expected of you in your first supervisory role is very different from the demands in a vice president role, for example. As your work purpose evolves, you, too, will grow and shift your behavior.

I had to learn this the hard way. Early in my career I received a promotion that forced me to change my behavior in order to survive and eventually excel. In my first 12 years in business, I was in operational roles in which I had line responsibilities. The way I saw it at the time was straightforward enough: I was the boss and could tell people what to do. After more than a decade, I was very comfortable in this type of leadership role. Then one day the chairman of the company promoted me to personnel director. This sounded like a cool job and came with a larger office. Sign me up!

At the outset I did not realize that this change of roles required a change of behavior on my part. I undertook my new responsibilities doing what I had always done: telling people what to do. Boom! I got my nose bloodied a couple of times before I realized that I could no longer "order" people to do certain tasks. I now had to learn to sell my thoughts and ideas. What an awakening.

The jump was more drastic than I imagined. I was in trouble and had to change quickly, so I made a list of which skills I should tone down, which I should pump up and which I had to learn fast. I identified the behaviors I had to change and committed then and there to making it happen or risk losing my new responsibilities. My humble but surprisingly effective plan looked like this:

> **Back off:** Stop telling people what to do; you are no longer their "boss"
> **Slow down:** Take time to build relationships
> **Ask questions:** Inquire regularly about important personnel topics
> **Really listen:** Carefully digest responses and keep notes for future use
> **Communicate effectively:** Craft your messages carefully and completely
> **Sell subtly:** Become a salesman for the right personnel policies

It took about six months for all of this to sink in and for my behavior to evolve to the point that I became truly effective. I think the company leaders saw I was making strides, and I appreciated the opportunity and leeway to make the necessary changes.

When you contemplate your own career, look to the future and consider how you and your role could evolve. In the role that you aspire to, how do the most successful people act? What do you see in the leaders you most respect that you could begin to practice yourself? Don't wait until you are in a tough situation like I did. Try to anticipate your future and make plans accordingly.

Job rotation builds your skills
2014

The best preparation for senior leadership roles is broad-based experience. Regardless of the strength of your skills, your growth potential will likely be limited when you stay in a narrowly focused role for a long time. Taking on different responsibilities gives you more knowledge and a deeper perspective on the organization. But it's up to you to take the initiative to serve in different roles.

My career began in retail store operations for a discount store chain in the Northeast. I volunteered to pitch in at grand openings during which I learned about operations on a different scale and I got exposure to senior leadership. I also volunteered for special projects, which led to being appointed to head the HR department. What a learning experience that was, going from line to staff management. All of a sudden, I had to learn how to "sell my ideas"—a pivotal new skill. It was tough and equally excellent preparation for future leadership positions.

In my second year at Tractor Supply, under a new president, I pitched in to take on several big ventures that were not in my area of responsibility. I learned about new parts of the business, plus I built a bond with the new boss. Six months later I was promoted to senior vice president.

My new role gave me responsibility over functions that I actually knew little about. But I quickly caught up. I went to an IBM school for managers of IT who have no technical background and then took an AMA course to learn more about accounting. I attended trade shows about logistics and studied marketing. Building this wide knowledge base was the best possible preparation I could have had to step into the role of president and later CEO.

The broader your experience base the better prepared you will be to take the next step into senior leadership. So don't sit back and rest on your laurels. Volunteer for special tasks. Talk to your boss about opportunities to move on to other responsibilities in the organization. Prepare yourself for growth by gaining wide-ranging experiences. Be proactive in building your career.

Start leading when you are young
NBJ Feb 21, 2014 (orig. Lead when you are young)

You'll benefit from being a leader early in life. Many of the best managers I know entered the world of leadership at a relatively young age. Becoming a leader in middle age may make it more difficult to build skills while managing the day-to-day. However, building your leadership reputation early on, when responsibilities outside of work don't add extra pressure, can get you way ahead of the game.

When I was in my mid-twenties, I managed approximately a hundred people operating the checkouts in a large discount store. This was a tremendous learning opportunity at a young age, and while I made a lot of mistakes I also matured in a hurry.

Here are some ways to take advantage of leadership opportunities:

- If you are in school, volunteer for leadership roles.
- Tell your boss that you are interested in a leadership role or are seeking leadership experiences.
- Push yourself into leadership roles by stepping up for tough assignments.
- Seek special tasks that will help you learn about different aspects of your organization and industry.
- Seek opportunities to build relationships and demonstrate your talents in front of senior executives, such as helping with the tough effort of opening a new retail store.

It's also beneficial to create a leadership learning agenda. Choose a variety of leadership books and magazine subscriptions. Then *schedule* your reading time. Likewise identify and attend industry events that make sense for your career development. Network with anyone and everyone (inside and outside your organization) who you think could help you become a better leader.

The skills to be successful in business are built over many years and come from myriad learning opportunities. Like any other skill, leadership can be learned by anyone with desire and drive. Jump in now—there's no advantage to waiting.

Get on a board!
NBJ August 3, 2018

Serving on a board—any board—is an opportunity to learn and grow in leadership. The benefits are vast:

You will develop and build relationships.

You will learn about a whole raft of different personalities.

You will be faced with a variety of problems to solve.

You will experience and have to deal with conflict.

You will overcome challenges you might never have thought possible.

I've been privileged to experience some of these career-enhancing board moments myself. After attending and making great contacts at several Retail Industry Leaders Association conferences, I was asked to join the organization's board, which includes many of the largest retailers in America.

Having a front-row seat on the RILA Board was a stellar opportunity to learn from my peers and to benchmark both my personal effectiveness and the effectiveness of my company. In fact, I learned more from those associations than almost most any other professional development during those years.

So how do you get started serving on a board? Start with these three questions:

What are your interests? Consider various non-profit boards, which are nearly always seeking help from good people. Look for organizations in which you have an interest and where your skills might be most beneficial. For example, if you want to help young people, look up the local Boys and Girls Club, your local charter school or other similar organizations.

What is your industry? Another place to seek out a board opportunity is in your trade or professional organization, where you could quickly prove a good fit. For example, I leveraged my position at Tractor Supply Company to serve on the Sponsor's Board of the FFA, formerly known as the Future Farmers of America. This opportunity allowed me to work with leaders from top agricultural firms while learning a great deal about both farming and leadership from a variety of new acquaintances.

Who do you know? Board opportunities can come from anywhere, so stay plugged in. When you are at a social or business networking event share business cards and ask questions. Effective networking is a key method to finding board positions. You can also fish around online. Study different organizations' websites to see if you already know someone in management or on the board. Then call your acquaintance to inquire about opportunities to serve on the board.

Even if you don't know someone, cold calling can demonstrate initiative. In fact, I remember receiving a cold call from a retail executive who admired Tractor Supply but had no contacts inside our company. He soon became a top-quality board member.

How to sell yourself: When you're in the position of having to demonstrate your worthiness to a board, take an inventory of your skills to assess where you might be of greatest benefit.

Boards are always looking for at least a couple financial people. Non-profits will see those with business-management skills as a real asset. And marketing and human resources skills are also attractive to most boards.

Then prepare a one-page profile of your skills and career background—a mini-resume—to present to the selection committee.

Once you're accepted, don't sit back studying all the personalities in the boardroom "laboratory." Jump in and demonstrate your worthiness—your ability to contribute in a meaningful way.

The benefits of board participation are well worth it. When you interact with other board members, your business skill base will grow as you grow.

So get on a board! Your career will thank you.

Navigating your new role at the top
NBJ December 27, 2013

With a new supervisory role come new responsibilities. There are two different approaches to getting started. Dive right in, offering direction on day one and letting the whole team know there's a new "sheriff" in town. Or take a few days, even weeks, to learn about your people and the unique aspects of your new business unit.

If you select the first option, as most people do, you will probably achieve some immediate results and have the confidence of knowing that you took charge quickly. Plus, *your* boss will probably appreciate your swift start. But while you may have firmly established yourself and rallied the team to follow your direction, you may have missed an important opportunity to really learn about your new responsibilities in an open environment.

Rather than a sprint, option two is methodical marathon. Pacing yourself allows you to spend some time learning on your new job. It will take a little longer to show results, but you could be leading from a much more solid position that could yield greater productivity in the long run.

If you can discipline yourself to try this method, start by spending individual time with everyone on your team. Your goal is to learn about each person and the history of your new business unit. Here are some questions to pose to employees that will lead to lively discussion and may help you better achieve your goals:

- What do like best about your job?
- What frustrates you at work?
- How would evaluate our business unit?
- What support can I provide to help you do your best?
- What advice would you give me to best lead our team?

This is your chance to get informed before you begin giving direction. At this point, withhold your opinions. Just listen. This is also an appropriate time to start building relationships by sharing a little about yourself—your commitment to strong values and a few stories about your family.

Early learning helps you understand business issues from the perspective of those doing the work. Getting to know your team first will help you appreciate what is important to each individual and lead more effectively.

Stand out in tough times
March 18, 2009

Tough economic times can be your time of opportunity. During tough times, organizations need effective leadership. You may have the title that makes you a leader, or you may simply be a leader amongst your peers. Regardless, this can be your time to shine.

You can choose the "ostrich route" by being scared and sticking your head in the sand, hoping for the storm to pass, or you can "step up" like never before. Ask yourself "What do I have to lose by accelerating my efforts at everything that can possibly help my company survive and excel?"

Assert yourself with enthusiastic support for your boss and the mission of your organization. Now is the opportunity to present your constructive ideas because your organization is probably more open than ever to finding new and better ways of doing business. You can contribute by being supportive of change. You can help morale by showing compassion and support for your fellow team members. Right now, you have everything to gain from being a "contributor."

Volunteer for "special assignments," particularly the really tough ones. Your boss is under more stress than usual and anything you can do to relieve that stress is good for you and your fellow team members. There is also a good possibility that a "special assignment" can lead to further responsibility and even recognition for going above and beyond. In these tough times, your boss will respect more than ever, those who step up to help by doing the following:

Be visible: Human nature leads us to lay low and keep our heads down when business is slow but the opposite is your best path. Move around your workplace, talk to everyone, listen carefully and be positive. Ask open-ended questions. You will be surprised at all of the ideas people have, that have not previously been expressed. Others will respect you for your communication and particularly your positive attitude.

Share information: Sharing is important during normal times, but it is even more important when times are tough. People perform best when they know the most. Be thorough, honest and right to the point on all communication. Uncertainty can lead to errors, confusion, frustration and even accidents. The more people know, the better they can perform. This is no time to keep secrets.

Recognize every act of good performance: Whether you are a manager or not, recognition is more important now than ever before. Catch people doing things right. Make it a point to always look for victories, no matter how small they may seem. Celebrate every success, acknowledge every win, and encourage new idea contribution. Keeping the team positive and enthusiastic relieves collective stress. You have everything to win and nothing to lose by building the spirits of everyone around you.

Assess your own performance and your contribution to your organization and if it is not up to standard, get it right today. Accelerate your time with the boss, try to differentiate your performance in a positive way and look to contribute constructive, new ideas.

While others may be scared of the future this is your time to shine. Ask yourself "What can I do personally to help my organization to do even better in these tough times?"

To mentor and to be mentored
NBJ March 2014

Several powerful mentors have helped me to grow and learn during my career. My dad was a business executive who taught me the inner workings of corporations from both a management and investment standpoint. In my career with Tractor Supply, my predecessor Tom Hennesy was my mentor for more than a decade. When I was an impetuous young man, he helped me evolve into a more mature leader. Tom also explained the importance of seeing the big picture and coached me in how strong values lead to the long-term success of the enterprise. Later, I mentored many young upward-bound leaders, and it's been one of the most rewarding experiences of my life.

Finding a mentor: First identify what you really want and need to learn; then narrow your focus to a few people that truly fit the profile. Study all you can about your target mentor—get to know that person as much as possible before taking the next step. When you are ready, simply tell your target, either in person or in writing, that you are seeking a mentor and would like to have a discussion.

Most leaders will feel honored and will likely schedule a meeting. Come prepared with your specific goals and a suggested schedule. I recommend one meeting a month at a neutral location. Assure your mentor that you will provide an agenda for each session.

Becoming a mentor: Jump at the chance—you will not regret it. If you have been in business for a while, you will have myriad experiences that can be helpful to young folks. You are in a respected position and have much more to share than you may realize. Consider using your successes and failures as tools; both can be instructional for emerging leaders.

I often find myself telling stories, good and bad, that shaped my career. And often my screw-ups are more important in the learning process than stories of success. If you accept a mentorship, I wouldn't be surprised if you become prouder of your mentoring than most anything else you are doing. A highly rewarding process, mentoring is an experience that fills both leaders and students with a great sense of pride and accomplishment.

Preparing for the world of work
NBJ December 2015

It's our obligation as adults, particularly parents, to help prepare the next generation for the big world ahead. And in an ever-changing workplace, that can require some serious career guidance. Everything business people do to coach and lead young adults in their search for rewarding careers is time well spent and will create lifelong memories—not to mention some very proud parents.

I had the pleasure of career-coaching one bright young man first-hand. When a close friend asked for my help in showing his son Michael the ropes in the business world, I enjoyed sharing my perspective during discussions with this aspiring entrepreneur, as well as showing him some Tractor Supply stores and even the boardroom. I could see his interest growing with each interaction. Michael decided on a business tract, went to college, earned a business degree and now in his late twenties has excelled way beyond his father's expectations.

Here are some ways we can all coach our youngsters in career choices.

Share experiences: Adult leaders who know how to share work experiences with young people in an authentic, non-threatening way can have enormous impact on their career choices. It is unusual for youth to know where they are going in life, so discussing our own struggles and successes can create real-life learning and, ideally, deeper interest and respect for the professional world.

Invite them inside: What's better than talking about workplace experiences? Getting youth inside an office, store or other place of employment. Let young adults check out your work place for a day by shadowing you or another leader. Experiencing a professional environment often works to pique a young person's interest in a specific career, job type or leadership position. It's easier to make a decision about a career when you can picture yourself in a credible day-to-day role.

Position opportunities: Some youngsters will head directly to college; others are best served by junior college or trade school. Likewise, it's our duty to guide specific students into careers that are a good fit, rather than a forced profession. Recently I traveled through a port city where I was amazed by a shipyard advertisement seeking 900 welders—good-paying, blue-collar jobs with an almost limitless demand for talent. The same can be said of our shortfall of quality technology professionals, and the demand for healthcare workers at just about every level seems never ending.

Start part-time: I started shoveling snow for a supermarket, graduated to cleaning out the stockroom and then on to operating a cash register. It was all uphill from there. I continually coach young folks to consider part-time work during their schooling. Regular work helps develop character and time management skills, while providing spending money and an early understanding of business functions that give job applicants a leg up. Plus, if you put your time in at low-paying, entry-level work in traditional industries like retail, restaurants and hotels, your patience and commitment could pay off in a surprisingly high-paying and rewarding long-term career.

Job search 101: Mentoring youth in finding quality jobs after completing education calls for an important reality check: Getting a job is a full-time job. One recent college graduate told me he sent out his resumes and was waiting for responses. That won't cut it in today's competitive work environment. Job seeking requires research, studying, mailing, networking, calling, knocking on doors and whole lot more.

If you've ever had a professional mentor, you know the value of career guidance. Maybe it's time to pay if forward—nothing could be more rewarding.

Thinking retirement? It's never too late to act now
NBJ April 2015

It's never too early to start preparing for retirement. Congress passed Social Security about 80 years ago to help seniors supplement the cost of retirement, and today there is much speculation about the long-term health of the program. In fact, it's nearly impossible to exist on Social Security alone. You have to create a more comprehensive financial plan to ensure you're as successful in life after work as you were during it.

My own story about the power of long-term saving might serve as an example. When Individual Retirement Accounts (IRAs) first came into existence in the late 1970s I started saving for retirement by contributing the annual maximum amount of $1,500, which I continued for three years.

Interest rates were very high so I invested in Certificates of Deposit (CDs) with my local bank and later in money market funds. When the maximum IRA contribution amount was later raised to $2,000, I contributed that maximum for the next 17 years, which means I invested a total of $38,500 over 20 years. When interest rates fell in the early 80s, I switched to a mutual fund that I still own today.

While this initial investment might not sound like much, when you save incrementally and refrain from withdrawing the growth can be tremendous. On an investment of $38,500 my results looked like this:

1990: $49,700
2000: $398,000
2010: $448,000
Today: $747,000

This example was all my money, but today most people have the option to participate in company-sponsored 401(k) retirement plans in which your employer matches a portion of your contribution, as much a 100 percent in some companies. Think about that. You put up a dollar and the boss kicks in another 50 cents or a dollar. What could be easier? And, remember, your contribution is in pre-tax money. The point is no matter what work plan you have, starting to save now for retirement will net you more money than you might think.

The key to success in retirement planning is to look long-term. A dollar put aside today might be $5 or even $20 by the time you retire. Small amounts grow well when invested intelligently—and left alone. If you are unsure about investment choices seek professional advice from a Certified Financial Planner, your banker or another trusted professional.

One more word of financial advice: Investments go up and go down. It's the nature of the game. So don't panic when markets fluctuate. That's what they do. The most critical components to retirement saving are regular contributions, solid growth investments, and, perhaps the hardest of all, not touching the account until you are ready to crash permanently on the beach.

Plan for retirement while still working
NBJ May 2011

We all hope to retire well. In our dreams, retirement may take the form of lazy days lying on the beach, playing golf or fishing. But in reality, if you are a typical Type A business leader like me you may have a hard time actually retiring.

For the first few months you may sleep late, eat on your own schedule and try to do all those things that you dreamt about over the years. But for most, the novelty of being retired wears off quickly, and you may find yourself looking for something more rewarding to fill your time.

After serving in a career that likely spanned more than 40 years and encompassed a series of challenging jobs and increasing responsibilities, a fair degree of job satisfaction, plenty of accomplishments and strong, long-term friendships, the shock of stopping work is a significant adjustment. Your sense of accomplishment may diminish and your old work buddies won't be as accessible. In effect, you will be faced with starting a new life.

So, what do you plan to do with the rest of your life? It's never too early to start developing a plan.

Scaling back: The path to retirement can be much smoother if there is a more limited or flexible role for you after your full-time career.

When my father retired at 65, he took a few weeks off and then went back to work three days a week doing essentially the same job for a different bank. Likewise, my brother-in-law retired a few years ago as a scientist at a large steel mill and returned to work as a consultant with his own flexible work schedule.

In my career at Tractor Supply Company, I spent a large portion of my time teaching and coaching store managers, district managers and executives. When I began to step down from a full-time career, I found an opportunity to pursue my passion for helping build the skills of business leaders through our leadership institute. Now I am doing what I love to do on a part-time basis.

As the population ages there are an increasing number of part-time, contract or consulting opportunities in a variety of industries.

Testing the waters: If you're not sure you want to simply scale back what you are currently doing in the business world, start exploring other options now. Get started by analyzing those things that interest you most. Ask yourself how you can get engaged in those topics in a meaningful way today.

Test everything you could possibly want to do before that final day arrives. For example, while you continue to work you can volunteer at a number of different non-profit organizations to see what type of work might be a good fit for your interests and skills.

Another fulfilling post-career role is teaching. You could try teaching occasionally on your topic of expertise. Again, you can test just about any retirement scenario while you are still working. The key is to start thinking about your options now so you have a real plan in place when your retirement arrives.

It is never too early to start planning the rest of your life. Right now, you may just be dreaming, but this will help you zero in on what might be best for you when the time arrives. Don't wait until you actually retire to start the process.

2. SKILLS

Want to be a leader? Start with these simple steps
NBJ 3/11/16 (Orig. Learning to lead)

Anyone with desire, common sense, an open mind and a positive attitude can learn to lead. That probably means you! Leadership is not complicated but it requires a different kind of hard work. Leaders are always learning; the cycle of constant improvement never stops. After 50 years in leadership roles, I am still learning every day. So how can you learn to lead?

Network: Consider every opportunity to observe leadership and then associate with the kinds of leaders you wish to emulate. Ask your friends and peers about the best leaders they know, and attend events that will expose you the widest variety of leaders. I found conventions and trade shows to be excellent opportunities to meet and listen to leaders. The professional associations I made at the leadership conferences of our retail trade organization, for example, helped me benchmark myself against some of the very finest retail executives.

Be inquisitive: If you know of good leaders in your community or industry, find ways to listen to them and study what they have done. Try cold calling, explaining your interests and asking politely for a few minutes of their time or a lunch date. When you meet, come prepared with an agenda for learning. Always be asking questions to learn more about leadership.

Read leadership books: Select four books a year—one per quarter. Educate yourself more broadly by selecting different topics and a range of authors. Select topics on which you know you need to improve. Then practice the skills you read about.

Stay informed and in tune: Informed leaders make the best decisions, so stay up to date. Regularly read general business trends and industry-specific articles. Make it easy by subscribing to *Forbes* or *Fortune* with the goal of reading an interesting article or two twice a week. When you have time pick up the *Wall Street Journal*. Also stay current with industry journals. Even schedule time for an educational seminar or online class once a year.

Trust your instincts: Many years ago, a mentor gave me advice that I draw on to this day: When theory says one thing and your gut tells you something else, go with your gut. This is particularly important when dealing with people and professional relationships.

Do the right thing: Walk the high road no matter the other influences. In the long run there is no substitute for integrity. Despite what is said or done by others, one of a leader's greatest gifts is to stand up for doing the right thing every time.

If you want to be a leader stay curious, keep learning and then throw your hat in the ring. Make your intent to be a leader known. You might be surprised by how quickly you can fill an empty spot at the top. Good luck.

First step for new supervisors: take a deep breath
NBJ November 24, 2016

Whether you've finally secured your dream CEO job or are just starting out in a junior-level leadership role, I advise you to take a deep breath before diving in. Most of us want to jump into our new role with both feet to show that we can get the job done as well or better than our predecessor. However, just the opposite approach might take you further. Slow down, because in the long run a measured approach could yield substantially better results for you and your organization.

If you assert yourself right away, setting direction and barking orders, you lose the opportunity to learn fully about your operation and your people. And without this basic knowledge you could easily stumble, maybe badly, due to a lack of ground-floor awareness. Here are some more tips for moving graciously into a new leadership role:

Be with the people: Remember, in most businesses those closest to the work know the most about it, so consider that your starting point. Spend time building a bond with people on the frontlines. This will pay off later in more ways than you can imagine. For example, in manufacturing, your mission is to walk the factory floor; in a sales role, go on calls with some of your people; and in retail, spend time in your stores and distribution centers. You get the idea.

Keep quiet and listen: During this initial learning period just observe, watch and pay attention—not everything is as it appears. Learn about the operations, challenges, problems and recent events. Then ask good questions about what you don't know. Likewise, get to know your people both professionally and personally. At this point you should begin to feel more comfortable with your team and they with you.

Learn all you can: Study all the facets of your new role: the history of your predecessors, culture of your company and your new business unit, and anything else that might help you better grasp the inner workings of your new position. This also includes reviewing the performance measures that you're expected to hit and counseling with the financial person who directly monitors your operation.

Start probing: After a reasonable time observing, you can start asking more substantial, in-depth questions that will help you do your job better. What are the big issues in the operation? If you were me what are the top three issues I should look into? How do you feel about the company overall? What do you see for yourself in the future?

If you follow this sequence of events roughly during your first few weeks in a new role, you should begin earning the respect of the workforce that you'll need for the future. So slow down long enough to get a solid understanding of the business and the people working for you, and ideally your team will rally around you—maybe even prevent you from making a mistake or two.

Leaders are always on stage!
NBJ August 2012

Business leaders are always on stage. As you interact with your team, customers, sales people, friends, family—even strangers—you send a message through everything you do and speak. People observe closely your words and actions as a leader. And most will follow your example, so make it good one.

First impression: This is important and lasting, so start things off right by dressing professionally. When in doubt, dress up one level. Set your sights on making a strong and positive impression every day on everyone you meet. Always send the message: I take pride in myself.

Simple smile: Everyone wants to be around positive, happy people. You can be that person by starting with a simple smile. When you smile, it changes your outlook, can lift your mood and instantly makes you a more approachable person. It even makes you more attractive. Like they say, smile and the world smiles with you.

Firm handshake: Bone-crushing handshakes are out, and wet dishrag handshakes communicate a lack of trust and a weak personality. Always remember that a firm handshake is a sign of strong character and personal confidence, regardless of gender. There is no gender in business.

Eye contact: This quickly communicates positive self-assuredness and demonstrates your interest in what another person is saying. Direct eye contact also keeps you focused on the person you are communicating with and minimizes distractions. "Look 'em in the eye" is the golden rule of one-to-one conversation.

Intentional listening: Listening is widely considered the most powerful communication skill—and one that we all can work on. Effective communication is directly related to the *quality* of our listening. When you listen, don't do it part way; do it intently. Despite the myriad tasks and important decisions running through your head, don't allow your mind to wander. Concentrate. Others will respect and admire you when you take time to *really* listen.

Crafted communication: Your communications skills are critical, so focus on the messages you deliver in every situation. Craft your words carefully to assure that you are giving clear, unambiguous direction. When you are in front of a group, speak professionally. Keep a good pace, but don't talk so fast that people can't follow your thoughts. Use good grammar. Be polite. Say "please" and "thank you" often. And, remember, there is no upside to using foul language.

Remember, you are on stage no matter where you are. Set the right example in and out of the workplace—in both words and deeds. There is a great deal of truth in the old adage that "your actions speak so loudly I can't hear what you say." Your image and your actions communicate everything about you, so make sure you are sending the message you want to send.

Focus on the important stuff!
NBJ January 2020

The most important words a mentor ever said to me were, "Don't confuse activity with accomplishment." He repeated this phrase so frequently that it's now burned into my brain. It makes so much sense.

He pointed out examples of unnecessary memos, wasted meetings and lost time on irrelevant topics. After a while, I began to plan my days and weeks with more laser focus and allocate my time for greater accomplishment. Once disciplined to make the best use of my time I could see myself actually getting more of the important stuff done. What an epiphany.

Here are some ways to start filtering out activities for accomplishment.

Understanding the measure of you: How does your direct report measure your performance? Knowing or revisiting the answer to this question will create immediate focus. Study your role carefully and ask yourself what accomplishment really looks like. Each morning, ask yourself: Am I focused on the issues that my boss sees as most significant? Am I planning my time for maximum results? Time is a limited resource and leaders need to plan it in a way that facilitates the best possible outcomes.

Managing time with a team: Leaders spend a big portion of time with their team, so make that time really count toward an end goal. Before your day gets underway or maybe the night before, plan out those interpersonal chunks of time and make notes about what you want to accomplish. When you are with your team, keep the conversation focused on topics that really count. A little social conversation is OK, but know when to cut it off. Keep the group's attention on the goals and measurements that will yield real success.

Focusing a business road trip: During a business trip to visit a retail store, I have observed supervisors who start a visit with a handshake, walk around the store, make a few comments and leave within 20 minutes. That's a perfect example of activity that yields little or no accomplishment. Spending a few hours in the store speaking with employees and customers, asking pinpointed questions and listening carefully is a much better path to learning. Only by uncovering the real issues and identifying new solutions to problems can your time result in any measurable success.

Dealing with email overload: Most of us feel constant pressure to read, digest and respond to emails. We can't stop this ubiquitous modern means of communication, so we need to learn how to minimize its distraction. First, use your digital tools. Hit the "unsubscribe" bottom at the bottom of any email distribution that's not essential. It's easy, and you can always re-subscribe. Also use "block sender" for those annoying repetitive emails. Try it for a week and you'll be surprised by how many fewer emails you receive. Second, discipline yourself to skim the first few lines of an email and quickly decide whether to delete or keep reading. Then flag priority emails so you'll remember to respond when you have time. Finally, if you are fortunate enough to have an assistant you can delegate email screening. Whether it's you or someone else, take charge of this function. Drive your digital communication; don't get yanked around by it.

Eliminating social media distractions: Unless your job role specifically deals with the monitoring or posting of your company's media messages, turn off or silence any social media notifications on your computer and phone. Allowing personal social media to dictate even parts of your workday, let alone your emotions, is a useless distraction. Stay focused on the real accomplishments you need to be successful. Keep social media off your agenda.

Cultivating work-life balance: Accomplishment is often amplified when you schedule restorative time for physical and mental health. By reducing useless activities during your workday, you should have more leeway to prioritize time for relationships and wellness. Schedule a weekly "date night" with your spouse. Build an achievable weekly exercise agenda. Plan quality time with your kids—experiences that uphold your values and make everyone feel accomplished. A solid work-life balance will create security and support for a successful business career.

It takes a lot of strength to stay focused on the most important issues without getting sidetracked by lesser activities. But it's worth the effort, and one day it will become routine. Fixating on a foundation for real accomplishment will take you down a lifelong path of success.

Be willing to listen more and you'll be able to lead better
NBJ December 2014

An open office door says you're open to communication. A closed door suggests you're closed off from the company conversation. The question is are you comfortable with people walking in to talk at any time? Do you need to hold "office hours"? As a leader it can be challenging to decide how to handle your open-door policy. But no matter how and when you do it, keeping your door open keeps the lines of communication open and makes you a more transparent, and therefore effective, leader.

The key is to commit to really receiving and listening to your visitors. It would be easy to stay parked behind your desk where you could see "urgent" emails popping up or paperwork that needs attention. But these distractions detract from the point of an open door in the first place. Your mind will be too scattered to concentrate on what matters: the concerns of your employees. Instead, make your in-office moments matter. Turn off your phone, silence the sounds from your terminal, and sit down in front of your desk to ensure an uninterrupted conversation.

Making dedicated time to listen is a key component of effective leadership. Good listeners earn respect from peers, subordinates and bosses. Plus, in most businesses the better you listen the more you'll learn which can help you make smarter decisions and provide the best direction for your business unit. Effective listening includes taking notes, asking questions, and then drilling down and following up on key topics. Equally it requires being open to all feedback, no matter how unpleasant.

Keeping an open door also means you can walk out of it. It might be a new concept, but try walking the halls at your business. You never who you will meet and what you might learn. During my regular hall walks at Tractor Supply, it was not unusual to see and touch new products, learn about a sick relative and hear a success story about customer service. "Wandering" helped me develop many fine relationships and kept me informed of a wide variety of issues.

Similarly, I spent half of my workweeks in stores and distribution centers listening and learning about every aspect of the business. I absorbed interesting information about stock levels—everything from critical replenishment issues to products our team thought we should carry. I also learned about product quality, packaging, assembly instructions and missing parts, plus operating processes that could be improved and even paperwork that could be simplified or eliminated. There is no limit to what you can learn by walking with and listening to those who are doing the work on front lines.

Listening, like any other skill, improves with time, effort and concentration. We can all develop our listening skills, and it starts with an open door. What better time than on the brink of a new year to set specific goals for becoming a better listener—and leader—in 2015?

"Are you listening? Some quick tips to open your ears"
NBJ April 2010

One skill that virtually all of us can improve is listening—*really* listening. Let's face it, most of us spend a large percentage of our waking hours listening to other people—spouses, family, coworkers and customers. That means we have a great opportunity to improve our skills in *quality* listening.

How many times has someone close to you been talking and interrupted your train of thought with the question, "Did you hear what I said?" And it is highly likely that we only heard a portion of what was said. It happens all the time. We are human, but we can improve. Here are some listening tips:

Concentrate: When we try to think about more than one thing at a time, we cannot possibly give our full attention to the person talking. The solution? Concentration. Don't allow your thoughts to wander. Focus on the person and the topic being discussed. You will quickly earn the respect of others by listening carefully and attentively.

Listen first with your eyes: Look at the speaker directly so you stay focused. Don't let your eyes (and thoughts) wander. And don't even consider your response until the person is finished expressing his thoughts. If you are busy formulating your next words, you are not listening. Focus on both the person and the message.

Question and engage: The message you are receiving is important to the person delivering it, and it may very well be of real benefit to you. If the message is not clear, ask for more information and clarification. Questioning and engaging in dialog helps you grasp the topic and confirm that you are really listening.

Remove distractions: Gain the respect of friends, family, customers and coworkers by taking the time to listen intently—and free of distractions. Put away the papers; shut off the phone; and focus on the person speaking. If someone comes to your office, sit in front of your desk facing your guest so that all distractions are behind you.

Make an appointment: Supervisors know that the best ideas come from those closest to the work, and therefore must be diligent about listening to every idea coming from team members. If someone wants to speak to you and you are busy, simply say, "I am busy right now. Let's set a time to discuss the topic." Then be sure you are there at the appointed time.

Focus on a tangible result: You can only provide the right solution for your customer after you listen carefully and thoroughly to fully understand their true needs, right? With this in mind, most high-achieving sales people will tell you that listening is their most important skill. Effective listening simply means more sales.

It takes a personal commitment and real concentration to become an outstanding listener, but there is no time like the present to put in place a personal development plan to really improve your listening practices.

Leadership means really listening
NBJ February 2015

After 50-plus years in business I have learned more through listening than any other practice. I have soaked in wisdom from executives, peers, subordinates, frontline workers, competitors and business partners. There is simply no limit to what leaders can learn through purposeful listening.

Looking back, I consider the time I spent listening to workers inside Tractor Supply stores invaluable. Team members talked to me about all they had learned and observed from customers. I heard about potential new products, ideas for improving operations, issues with inventory replenishment and even opportunities for new store locations. Listening wasn't that hard, but it worked like magic.

However, there are so many things that can get in the way of good listening in a business setting. Start your listening exercises by moving these common obstacles out of the way first:

> ➤ Manually shut off the phone, terminal and other potential distractions.

- Get out from behind your desk to talk (and listen) face-to-face.
- Concentrate on just listening! Learn to ignore surrounding interruptions.

Then conduct your listening in a professional manner and work to control potential impediments to good listening. Let's start with a list of what *not* to do:

- Don't let stiff or guarded body language send the wrong message.
- Don't look around at other distractions. Make sustained eye contact.
- Don't prejudge, no matter your personal thoughts and experiences.
- Don't let emotions enter the process. Try to remain a neutral information collector.
- Don't disagree until thoughts are complete; then clarify with thoughtful questions.

Now on to the "do" list for more effective listening:

- Stay focused on the conversation at hand. Try to keep your mind from wandering.
- Listen 75% of the time; talk intelligently 25%.
- Ask probing questions for better understanding, but only when socially appropriate.
- Stay on topic. It's better to hear a lot about one topic than a little about a dozen.
- If you have a thought, don't interrupt. Make a note to discuss it later in the conversation.

For those really important conversations, make sure you're extra prepared to listen well by reviewing past notes and current reports. Write down in advance your key thoughts, ideas and potential questions to ask. If you ever have a disagreement about a fact, stop and look it up. Debating details can be a waste of time and emotion.

It's easy to see why good listeners are often perceived as more intelligent—they probably are! Listening allows us to learn more richly about more subjects and use this knowledge to become more effective leaders. Over time good listeners earn greater respect from associates and build a stronger reputation within an organization. Maybe it's time to stop talking—and begin focusing on the art of listening.

Being busy not a sign of being effective
NBJ February 2013 (Original title: Don't Confuse Activity with Accomplishment)

Don't confuse activity with accomplishment. Fifty years ago, my first mentor told me that simple phrase—and it's helped me be a better leader ever since.

Young, active and energetic, I worked for a large discount store in New Jersey, where I was responsible for a bank of 20 checkouts and supporting functions. On Saturday mornings, our busiest time of the week, my boss's boss often dropped in to observe.

Then he'd have me sit down for coffee, pointing out how many places I had been in the last 30 minutes, performing trivial chores that I could easily delegate. He helped me focus on the important stuff—selecting good people, coaching my team and planning for the next several weeks. I was a slow learner, but it finally sank in: Busyness and business are not the same things.

Acting—not just looking—the part: Here's an example of how to separate activity and accomplishment. At Tractor Supply, we had managers who were fanatical about maintaining a picture-perfect store. They would work extra hours to ensure every display was neat and every shelf was precisely organized to meet every company standard. While it sounds like a very practical goal, strong leaders know this is *not* the most important ingredient in the most successful stores.

The best sales and profits come from stores with an overriding passion for first-class customer service—the places where employees jump through hoops to make sure every customer is satisfied. In fact, when I would call to praise these outstanding stores, it was not unusual for the manager to say, "Sorry, Joe, but I can't talk right now. We have customers to take care of." These leaders are focusing on the right thing. Creating a flawless store is a time-consuming activity; delivering stellar customer service is the key to maximum accomplishment.

This message translates to all businesses. We can all learn the tasks that lead to the greatest accomplishment in our own lines of work. In most cases, accomplishment is tied directly to increasing revenues and profits. As you think about your role in your organization, try to step back and analyze your daily activities to assess how they align with the factors that lead to true accomplishment.

If your employees are frantically replying to every email that pops in the inbox, thinking that the sheer act of answering each and every correspondence is an accomplishment, help them think outside the inbox. As a leader, you should clearly define for your team the actions that lead to real, productive accomplishment—not just activity.

Network your way to success
NBJ July 2014

Networking builds business knowledge and enduring friendships. I've been retired for a half dozen years and still have strong ties with scores of former business associates. Don't be shy—get going—networking is a winning formula for personal development. Here are a few key ways to get engaged:

Industry associations: In my last 20 years in business, I learned more from my professional associations than any other single source. Spending time with my peers—the leaders of other retail companies—helped me learn in myriad ways. It also helped me judge both my personal performance and that of my company.

Your company: Reinstate the daily meet-and-greet. Get to know those in other parts of your own organization. Coffee, lunch, mini meetings in the hallways—do whatever it takes to build relationships throughout your company.

Competitors: An occasional conversation with a competitor can do wonders to benchmark your company and your personal skills. There are plenty of non-competitive issues on which you can collaborate with the competition—sometimes to the benefit of your entire industry.

Trade shows: Most of us have the opportunity to attend shows about the products and services in our field. This is a great opportunity to meet others, build beneficial relationships and learn about the latest trends in your industry. Maximize your time by setting up short sessions with the top players in your game.

Local events: The Nashville Business Journal puts on near-weekly events. Take advantage of local business events like these to make new acquaintances. You can also join a non-profit to help in the community and grow your contact base. You might just find some new customers among your new contacts.

Friends: Keep in touch with your friends near and far. Staying connected boosts self-confidence and can be a surprising source of knowledge on a wide range of topics.

Remember, networking is about learning *and* growing. The broader your network the more you will learn. The more people you network with the more interesting person you will grow into. Get engaged today.

Networking means knowledge, success
NBJ August 2013

Building your own personal brand requires a large network of professional associates, peers and friends. Think of every person you meet as an opportunity to learn something new. The more people you associate with the greater your chances to build your knowledge base. And the bigger your knowledge base the greater your likelihood of success.

My 20-year involvement with Tractor Supply Company's retail trade organization allowed me to spend time with peers who ran a large retail company. Through these associations I observed and learned a variety of leadership styles and how to benchmark both my company and myself against some of the best in the business. This form of networking was one of my principal methods of learning and improving.

I continue to network today, recently engaging an acquaintance at a cocktail party to work with a local non-profit I support. It only took trading business cards and a short follow-up to seal the deal. Another simple exchange has led to public speaking opportunities. Not all social events are this productive, but you never know until you try. Here are few more networking tips I've learned along the way:

Make lunch count: Have lunch with as many different people as you can. Every mealtime and break time is opportunity time—don't let it go to waste. Avoid routine daily lunch with same people—or at your desk.

Keep track: Never leave home without business cards in your pocket. When you meet someone new, exchange cards and then quickly follow up, preferably with a good, old-fashioned handwritten note. Be sure to log every new association in your contacts file.

Reach out: Take the initiative to call, email and occasionally schedule face time with the contacts you think have the most potential. It's impossible to imagine all the ways reaching out can benefit you.

Cold call: It sounds scary, but you will find that most people respond positively to a cold call from a peer and often respect the initiative. This is easiest when the industry, company or individual has recently been in the news. Try it. You might be surprised by how well cold calling actually works.

Networking is your opportunity to learn. The more associations you make, the more you learn and the more valuable, worldly, interesting, and I believe, happier, you become.

Network your way to success
NBJ July 2014

Networking builds business knowledge and enduring friendships. I've been retired for a half dozen years and still have strong ties with scores of former business associates. Don't be shy—get going—networking is a winning formula for personal development. Here are a few key ways to get engaged:

- **Industry associations:** In my last 20 years in business, I learned more from my professional associations than any other single source. Spending time with my peers—the leaders of other retail companies—helped me learn in myriad ways. It also helped me judge both my personal performance and that of my company.
- **Your company:** Reinstate the daily meet-and-greet. Get to know those in other parts of your own organization. Coffee, lunch, mini meetings in the hallways—do whatever it takes to build relationships throughout your company.
- **Competitors:** An occasional conversation with a competitor can do wonders to benchmark your company and your personal skills. There are plenty of non-competitive issues on which you can collaborate with the competition—sometimes to the benefit of your entire industry.
- **Trade shows:** Most of us have the opportunity to attend shows about the products and services in our field. This is a great opportunity to meet others, build beneficial relationships and learn about the latest trends in your industry. Maximize your time by setting up short sessions with the top players in your game.
- **Local events:** The Nashville Business Journal puts on near-weekly events. Take advantage of local business events like these to make new acquaintances. You can also join a non-profit to help in the community and grow your contact base. You might just find some new customers among your new contacts.
- **Friends:** Keep in touch with your friends near and far. Staying connected boosts self-confidence and can be a surprising source of knowledge on a wide range of topics.

Remember, networking is about learning *and* growing. The broader your network the more you will learn. The more people you network with the more interesting person you will grow into. Get engaged today.

Simplicity is a winning formula
NBJ September 2022

We've all heard the expression KISS: "Keep it simple stupid." The point? If you can get your message across in a sentence don't use a paragraph. KISS applies to all aspects of life, including the business world.

To best lead your team, edit directions to essential information—what's necessary to get the job done. Review the crucial data and required tools, but don't dive into extraneous topics. Excessive details may only confuse the process.

Verbal directions: In the spirit of simplicity, let's use a basic building example to demonstrate how simple, pro-active verbal instructions can minimize misunderstandings and increase productivity:

- The big picture is that we're going to build a 2-mile fence along Highway 29
- Today's goal is to build the next half mile in the project
- Materials have been placed at intervals along the fence path
- We will break for a 30-minute lunch at noon
- Completion is scheduled for 4 p.m.
- Before we get started, do you have the tools you need? What other questions can I answer?
- I will be available here or near all day—you have my number.

Written communications: The same KISS strategy works for written communications. My favorite? Bullet points. Short descriptors as opposed to long-winded paragraphs keep readers engaged and informed. Again, keeping communication simple can help clarify and streamline any business process.

KISS is also worth considering when building a resume or mentoring someone in this critical career aspect. For example, I recently came across a three-page, single-spaced, small-font resume. Very few recruiters, who are scanning scores of resumes, will take the time to read three pages.

A resume is your advertising flyer so it needs to quickly sell your key skills and background. Headlines and highlights in one intentional, immaculate page can garner just enough interest. An interview is the time to discuss experience in detail.

Consider the "end user:" When you communicate "up the ladder" in business, overly complex communications can become a turn off instead of a successful sales pitch. It's important to consider the end user—who's hearing, reading or digesting this content?

My dishwasher instruction manual is a model case of excess: It's 24 pages of microscopic type. There's probably enough information for me to build my own dishwasher. And guess where the operational instructions are located? Page 24.

When communicating with your team, think about how frustrated you feel going through an unwieldy appliance manual. It's up to you to guide the communication. Any good idea can be communicated on one page. My team always knew one page was the limit. Details come later, once the idea is accepted.

As a general rule, leaders should put both written and verbal communication in the simplest possible context. KISS—keep it simple stupid—is the smartest way to earn respect from your team.

Sharing the secret to building trust
NBJ June 2014

What's the secret to building trust in business? Sharing. As my mentor Tom Hennesy taught me, collaboration is key. Being protective and defensive about information can actually erode trust over time. Sharing, on the other hand, leverages everyone's strengths, creating an environment of respect, commitment, support, and, most importantly, trust.

This idea crystalized for me as I recalled a time as young boy when my parents shared with me their budget for new dining-room furniture. All of a sudden, I really felt important and included—and I immediately wanted track down a fine set for just the right price. Sharing made me part of the family team.

Unfortunately, many leaders maintain a mindset of sharing "only what they need to know." In this culture of secrecy, team members wonder: Is something bad going to happen? Are we in trouble? And these are the questions that take focus off work, often leading to declining productivity and morale.

Fortunately, the simple act of sharing can build back trust. Here are some examples of how sharing has led to better business at Tractor Supply Company.

> **Sharing for action:** Many years ago, when I delivered my first comprehensive vision speech to our corporate leaders, I shared information about all the key operating units and how we could work as a team for mutual success. I held nothing back. Starting that day, eyes were opened, people started asking questions and action ensued.
>
> **Sharing for camaraderie:** At our company, monthly team bonuses are based on sales, so to encourage healthy competition and camaraderie, we post daily sales results in break rooms. It's obvious how each team is doing and who's not pulling a fair share. But it's also clear that collaboration and team dynamics are at the heart of every company's success.
>
> **Sharing with customers:** Each year, two hundred of our largest merchandise suppliers attend a vendor conference, where we share information about growth, marketing, strategies, and just about anything we think will help our

customers best fit into a winning partnership. I'm convinced that we all win when we work closely together.

You can start today: Pledge to begin sharing important information with your people. As you empower your team members, more decisions will come off your back, while you build a new culture of trust.

Promote yourself but don't brag
NBJ January 2019

"It is good to do good in the community. And it is also good to be known for doing good." A wise mentor of mine uttered these words many years ago when discussing a community initiative at Tractor Supply. I never forgot this declaration. When we make a contribution of any kind to our business or community it is human nature to yearn for a little credit. To put it another way, we all want recognition for doing good. It feels good.

However, bragging is a different thing altogether. Folks who drone on and on about personal accomplishments or name drop in a futile attempt to stand out eventually isolate themselves. Why? Because braggarts are boring. On the flipside, some people never toot their own horn. That's not the best solution either. There's a careful balance that will help determine your success as a leader.

Follow this roadmap to pave your career path in a positive way.

- ➢ **Build a bond with your boss:** Talk about your ambitions. Ask for advice and guidance. Most superiors would be happy to see you be even more successful. Remember, it could be a feather in your leader's cap, too. Your boss could easily become your No. 1 promoter.
- ➢ **Volunteer for tough assignments:** Take on hard projects with confidence and follow through. You will get noticed, and these assignments can often lead to bigger, better opportunities.

- **Branch beyond your bubble.** Attend events that help your skill base—and your contact list. Make a list of important trade shows, industry classes, seminars, etc. that could help your cause.
- **Network in your company:** You don't have to attend an industry event to grow your network. Start by building solid relationships with your peers and in other parts of the organization. Have lunch once and a while and discuss big-picture issues with an eye on the future.
- **Meet your business community:** Stepping out to share business cards, thoughts and ideas with peers and business leaders still works wonders. And you will be surprised by how eager acquaintances are to help when asked.
- **Ask for the intro:** If during a conversation someone mentions the name of a person you would like to meet, go ahead and ask for an introduction. It's not considered too forward in a professional environment. Go for it.
- **Share others' successes:** Always speak well of others on your team and in your company. Share the accomplishments of your peers and competitors.
- **Stand up for the right values:** Always walk the high road in every situation, both personally and professionally.
- **Become a good public speaker:** It can be hard to motivate for something that "puts you out there," but I promise public speaking pays off. You will get better with practice.
- **Just smile:** Even the act of smiling can put you (and others!) in a more positive, productive mindset. Be friendly, and always conduct yourself with an "I have no enemies" attitude.

Building solid relationships is an important step in gaining positive exposure. Stay humble, but don't be afraid to share your accomplishments. You deserve the respect you've earned.

Thank you, Dr. Brain Surgeon
NBJ December 2012

I learned something important last summer. A casual acquaintance, who I bonded with over home building, told me he was a brain surgeon. I was fascinated by his profession until he said something that struck a chord deep in my professional psyche. He said that he saves lives on a regular basis, yet no one ever thanks him. I was shocked. Can you imagine mending brains for a living and never getting a pat on the back?

I decided to use what I had learned for some greater good. First, I called the doctor who repaired my torn meniscus a year earlier to thank him for doing a good job. My knee works great. He seemed dumb-founded by the call. Then I thought about the importance of recognition in all workplaces—and for all employees.

A chain reaction: Recognition has surprising and long-lasting benefits. We react positively when someone praises us constructively for something we have accomplished. It's pretty simple: Give him a self-esteem-boosting pat on the back and he will do more, and probably better. Present her with an award in front of her peers and she will become your biggest supporter. Add family to the mix and an employee might just be in your court for life.

In our leadership classes we often discuss how to positively impact employee performance in both good and bad circumstances. There is always consensus that recognition is the one universal factor that has no downside and almost always yields a positive impact on performance. Here are a few ways to start incorporating more gratitude in your life and work:

- First, ask yourself, how often you have sincerely thanked a professional who has helped you.
- Second, try to draw on how you felt personally the last time you were recognized for doing a good job in your professional life.

- Next, take few minutes from time to time to thank those that help you but seldom get recognized. Maybe start with one extra thanks a day and build from there.
- Finally, reap your own reward: It just feels good to have gone the extra mile for someone who may seldom get credit for a job well done.

It only takes a minute or two to give credit where it's due. You might make someone's day—and just maybe your own.

Recognize good work to motivate employees
NBJ March 2011

Just look into the eyes of someone who has been recognized for a job well done. They shine. As my mentor and former CEO Tom Hennesy always said: Recognition is the number one motivator of people.

As a business leader, if you consistently recognize good behavior, you are likely to get a lot more of the same behavior. A sincere pat on the back takes just a few seconds and can have enormous impact on attitude and performance—and there is absolutely no risk involved.

Give—and receive—earnest recognition: If you have the opportunity to congratulate someone in front of others, it has even greater significance. Offering a team member sincere appreciation for hard work will in turn earn you greater respect as a leader and, ultimately, enhance your image among other employees.

When face-to-face communications are difficult, for example if you are responsible for the operations in multiple locations, make it a habit to call the managers and supervisors who achieve big successes. You can also use your call wisely to gather key business feedback. Start your conversation by discussing day-to-day operations, and conclude by congratulating the manager and the whole team. Managers will be excited to hear from the boss, and you will learn a few things about how to better support your operations in other locations.

Don't be afraid to celebrate success: Meetings are a perfect time to recognize and celebrate success. Even in a small, routine meeting you can usually find something—and someone—to recognize. When you start off on a positive note meetings often run more smoothly. Likewise, large sales gatherings should always be a time for recognizing the best performers. The more you take the appropriate time to celebrate individual successes, the more people will strive to achieve that same level of success.

Share success through storytelling: Telling success stories is an engaging method of recognition and education. Get in the habit of passing on success stories at every opportunity, and if your team is spread out geographically, circulate those stories in writing. When you share success stories, you are recognizing both an individual for accomplishment and a larger team achievement. In addition, others will learn from the success story about how they might achieve a similar result.

We all win by giving recognition. First, everyone feels more positive in a recognition-driven culture. Second, recognition reinforces desired behavior. Finally, leaders who provide sincere recognition earn the respect and admiration of the whole team.

Why don't you ask more questions?
NBJ March 2020

When interviewing potential team members, the trait of curiosity was always near the top of my list. Why? Curious individuals often come up with the most innovative and even breakthrough ideas that can make a real difference in business. Curious people probe and ask the questions that can make some leaders feel a little uncomfortable. And that's OK, too.

My attitude is, bring it on! We need thought-provoking team players that challenge the status quo. That's the only way to move the needle. Here's how to get more curious every day.

Practice inquisitive thinking: Don't just take the things you see, hear and experience in the workplace at face value. Instead, explore, investigate and observe. Probe for reasons and understanding. Ask harder questions. Experts suggest that curiosity is a driving force in human development. In the business world curiosity is compounded; it's an essential leadership skill.

Converse with curiosity: Start conversations with a mindset of curiosity. When something is of interest to you or appears important to the other person don't let the subject die. Listen well so you can probe further with your own insightful questions. Ask more—how, why, where, when, etc. Every conversation can evolve your education, strengthen friendships and lead to future connections.

Be a good interviewer: Prepare for each interview with a handful of key topics and a curiously positive attitude. Watch how one question can lead to another. When a candidate speaks of a particular success, drill down deeply to understand the key factors that drove that success. You'll get a clearer picture of a candidate by spending more time on a few really important topics rather than checking off every box on a standard questionnaire.

Make friends with change: They say the only constant in life is change. But most people fear change, and the bigger the change the greater the fear. But this is the time to be ultra-curious. Because the more you understand about the changes coming at you in business the better you will be able to cope with and execute on a new goal. It's particularly important to understand big-picture goals, the methods of measurement and the real reasons behind change. So, study up and then ask every logical question you can.

Get to know people better: The workplace is not the only place that curiosity can lead to good things. Try it at home. For example, kids are naturally curious about the world but they also like it when other people are curious about them. When you ask questions or share your own experiences about being a kid or teen once, too, they will eventually open up. But practice consistently—a free-flowing session each night—and don't be afraid to change your inquiry style. They'll come around, and your relationship will be stronger for it.

Become more interesting: It sounds silly, but being curious makes you a smarter, more interesting person. When you can ask good questions and show genuine interest in others' lives, people will gravitate toward you. We all feel good when we can talk about what's important in our own life and spark a connection with someone. Curiosity is an admirable attribute: it earns you respect, strengthens your friendships and makes your life infinitely more interesting.

That catchphrase "curiosity killed the cat" doesn't hold up for humans. In fact, we're more alive because of it.

Effective leaders are also strong salespeople
NBJ 3-12 (Orig. We Are All Salespeople)

On your first job interview you became a salesperson—for yourself. Your resume is your personal sales brochure. Every interview question is an opportunity to sell yourself. We are, after all, distinct individuals with our own unique appearances, personalities and combination of traits that make us special. Throughout life we will all be in one way or another selling ourselves.

From the time you had your first bright idea at work and pushed it forward, you were selling what you believed in. When you submitted your big project report you sold to your boss all the work that you and your team accomplished. As a senior leader you might be selling your thoughts and expertise to the board of directors.

Salesmanship remains a key component of leadership. I learned to hone this skill quickly during one enlightening job change. For the first 12 years of my career, I was a line manager, giving orders and often selling objectives to my team. But I was the boss. Then I was given the role of Personnel Director, a position with a lot of responsibility but only a tiny staff. Now I was in a position where I had to use my sales skills to convince managers and executives about all the issues of managing people. Suddenly, in order to get things done I was forced to become a very effective sales person.

Just as I convinced my leaders of personnel needs, successfully completing the business mission means convincing, persuading and selling your team on the direction you have set. You may know more about the details, but it is your sales ability to get your team moving in the right direction that translates into success. The more successfully you sell your plan, the more committed your team will be, which in turn will yield the best possible results.

As you grow in your business leadership role your skills of persuasion will become increasingly important. Selling the vision of a business unit is a common and crucial talent of successful executives. No matter where you are in your career it is never too late to work on building stronger sales skills.

Time is a limited, nonrenewable resource; take control of yours
Aug 30, 2013, NBJ; (Orig. Take control of your time)

You can't replace time, so make the most what you have. This probably sounds like something your mom would say. And you're probably saying to yourself, "I'm slammed with work and may never dig out." The good news is we can all get a grip on personal time management. Here are some things that have worked for me:

- ➢ Take charge of your calendar. Don't let others set your agenda!
- ➢ Confirm times and agendas of meetings and appointments a day or two ahead.
- ➢ Practice saying no. Ask for the objective of an appointment or meeting, and request a summary of the objectives before you say yes. Get tough—it's your time.
- ➢ Schedule personal time first and way in advance. Block out vacation and important family events time at least six months ahead.
- ➢ If you're in charge of a meeting, take charge. Set and share the agenda, ask for feedback and establish times for each agenda topic. Then politely keep folks on task and on time.
- ➢ If you're not running the meeting, show up on time and politely challenge those who don't. Request the agenda and the time schedule. Consider leaving at the scheduled ending time regardless of the status of the meeting. You may just set a new standard.

> Show respect for other people's time. That means being prompt for everything and not tolerating tardiness from anyone on your team.
> Set specific "think time" for yourself. Find a quiet spot, preferably off premises, where you can do some deep thinking about the long-term health of your business unit and your career.

At this point you may be saying this is all good advice but my boss is always calling impromptu meetings that mess up my carefully scheduled plans. Don't give up—there may be a solution. First explain to your boss in a logical, factual way how your sense of organization and time management leads you to solid results. One discussion may not do it, but regular calm talks might just help your higher up see the light.

Remember, time is valuable and non-renewable. Take charge to make the most productive use of the time you have.

Joe Scarlett is the retired CEO of Tractor Supply Co.
He can be reached at Joe@joescarlett.com

Executive advice: build your public speaking skills
NBJ—July 2022

It's well documented that public speaking is among our greatest fears. Most people actively avoid making speeches—and those that do muster the courage typically struggle with nervousness leading up to a big talk. But if you want to grow in your leadership role this is one skill that you will have to master.

I have been speaking in public for more than 50 years and to this day I'm still not perfectly comfortable in front of a group. I still experience a certain amount of stress whether I'm talking to 10 people or 1,000 people. But I have gotten used to managing this temporary uncomfortableness—and so can you.

Practice is your best friend for becoming a better public speaker. Delivering a speech is like any other skill in life—the more you do it the better your skills will become. My advice is to take every possible opportunity you can to speak in public, no matter what the venue. There's no time like the present to get started facing this universal fear.

10 tips for better public speaking: Preparation and practice are essential components to your public speaking success.

1. Only commit to speaking on topics that you really know and understand. My two worst speeches were on topics selected for me, but not in my wheelhouse.
2. Keep your topic focused on a few key points—too many topics in one speech can confuse the audience.
3. Start with a bulleted outline, but use whatever words that come to mind to keep your talk conversational and engaging. Avoid reading speeches; this may come across as staged and insincere.
4. Review and revise your notes so you are comfortable with the flow of the speech when the day arrives.
5. Practice as much as you can. Speak in front of a mirror, use a recorder and maybe have a friend listen to you. The best teacher of all is watching yourself on a video (before and after your speech).
6. Visit the venue well ahead of your speech so that you are comfortable with the surroundings.
7. If possible, mingle with the audience before your talk so you can make eye contact with a few friendly faces during your speech.
8. If you are using PowerPoint or any other support materials, make sure all is in working order ahead of time.
9. Discipline yourself to speak slowly. Nerves can cause us to race through our speech, but a measured cadence will always lead to better comprehension of the message.
10. Dress professionally—the audience is listening, but they are also watching.

Find a coach: Another great way to get over the fear of public speaking is to seek out coaching wherever you can find it. A great example: Prior to a selling tour to take our company public, my team was invited to spend time with a speaking coach in New York. We thought we had a great pitch, but after watching ourselves on video it became clear we needed help. By the end of the day our slide deck went from 40 slides to 10—and our spoken words were crisp and right on target. Bottom line: Our stock offering was oversubscribed by a factor of six! The coaching was well worth it.

Not sure where to start? Draft your own coach: A lot of business executives are more than happy to work with willing students. Just ask!

Delivering an effective speech among audiences of all sizes is an essential business leadership skill. As you are working your way up the ladder, do everything in your power to build and refine critical verbal skills. You won't believe the doors that open when you become a more confident speaker.

Returning calls, emails not just polite
NBJ October 2012 (Orig. Build a positive reputation)

Reputation is direct reflection of you. It is impacted by everything you say and do—but also by what you *don't* say and do.

Take this recent example: A customer of ours was having trouble getting approval for expensive, high-demand class instructors from out of town. We suspected an issue but couldn't get a response to our repeated calls and emails. In the end, we canceled the instructors late in game, hoping that they could re-book their time. This intentional avoidance of communication is a sure-fire path to a poor reputation.

In another ongoing case, a particular company vice president never takes the time to return phone calls. Sadly, his reputation for ignoring the most basic of communication skills—responding to calls, requests and emails—has become his calling card. Most people don't even waste time making contact anymore. Just like "hiding" from an uncomfortable situation by not communicating, ignoring people and disrespecting their time will undermine your reputation.

If you avoid or ignore people, they're not the only ones that lose out. Think of what you might be missing out on too: important business information, networking to grow your knowledge base, a once-in-a lifetime job opportunity, a great investment or even a chance to make a new friend.

The key to keeping your reputation in check is to communicate early and often. Be proactive in how you choose to deal with people. Have the courtesy (and a strategy) to return regular communications. Quite simply, the path to a positive reputation is strong, straightforward communication.

Getting along with the boss
NBJ November 2018

The relationship you have with your boss is one of the most important in your daily life. To be honest, it probably ranks right behind the one you have with a spouse or significant other. In part that's due to the sheer amount of time you spend on the job. But it's also the meaning behind the relationship: your earning potential depends on it.

Getting along with your boss is big business. And it rests squarely on your shoulders. I know. Early in my career I was given lots of responsibility, leading more than 50 employees and proving to my boss that I could deliver.

I learned very quickly that having a solid rapport with my boss was good for peace of mind and great for my career. Here are a few thoughts on making this relationship work:

Build a sturdy communications bridge: Figure out the best communication style for your professional relationship. Work it out together. Find the answers to questions like: How frequently should we meet? Better to have one longer weekly meeting or short daily ones? Want just the headlines or details? Get real clarification as early as you can in the relationship.

Help your boss achieve: Every leader wants to win in business. We all want to succeed. Learn the key measures of success in your work group and help the team (and subsequently your boss) shine. When your group meets or exceeds goals, life is good for everyone.

Limit important communications: When you are talking or writing to your boss keep communication focused no more than two or three key points. It's hard to get real attention on more than a few topics at once, so you'll help the relationship by keeping things focused

Define standards of written materials: Does the boss want detailed reports or bulleted memos? How much research or backup material is necessary? A friend once put it this way: "Does the boss want to know what time it is or does he/she want to learn to build a clock?"

Agree to disagree: Your thoughts and ideas are valuable, and bosses need to hear all sides of the important issues. Be careful, be respectful, be calm. When you want to present a different point of view, chose the time and venue carefully. And don't get into these discussions at times of high stress.

Always support your boss: Get behind the boss in every way you can. Negative remarks always boomerang and will give you one big black eye. Be positive—it always pays off! If you do encounter issues, approach your boss proactively, rather than stewing and saying something you shouldn't to the wrong person.

What motivates your boss?: Maybe he/she is big on punctuality. If so, be on time—all the time. Maybe he/she dotes on grandchildren or values family above all. If so, don't forget to comment on life outside work. Maybe your boss reads a lot. So, recommend a book. Figure out what motivates your boss and make it work to your benefit.

Be a coach and teacher: Leaders respect those who do the most to develop the team. Take every opportunity you can to help others build their job skills. Initiatives like this sit well with the boss and encourage respect among your peers.

Toot your own horn occasionally: It's just fine to let your boss or others know about your accomplishments—tastefully. Stay humble, stay accurate and don't sound like a braggadocio.

Every boss is different, which means we must learn how best to adapt. Remember, as you grow in your career your boss is also growing. Think of every interaction as an opportunity to learn and evolve. In the process, you might even help your boss in become a better leader.

Your health key to business
NBJ April 20, 2012 (Orig. Take Care of Yourself, Take Care of Business)

"Take care of yourself, exercise, eat the right food and be careful." Most of us can still hear our parents saying these exact words. We give the same advice to our children. But following these lessons personally can give you an edge in your professional career as well.

Be your own boss: Stress creates myriad psychological issues and manifests itself in many ways physiologically. Basic stress management is up to you—no one else. You are in charge of your mind and body. You are your own boss. Plan carefully, delegate generously and know when to stop. When stress levels are high, communicate often and calmly. Sometimes just "talking it out" can put things in a more realistic perspective.

Get moving: Taking care of yourself physically can reduce stress at work and likely help you live a little longer. When you take care of yourself you may discover an inner confidence through outward physical strength. You will be able to work harder, longer (and maybe faster), and deal more effectively with stress. A regimen of physical exercise can improve your energy level and mental stamina throughout the day, helping you remain calm in tense situations and deal better with business issues, big or small. So, walk, run, swim, play team sports or work out at the gym. Do whatever you like, but do something.

Invest in health: Once you hit your thirties an annual physical is an investment in your future health. You review business reports all the time. Why shouldn't you review critical reports on your health regularly? We all know someone who has ignored a minor nagging problem and avoided a trip to the doctor—until was too late. Or others, who like me, may have smoked two packs a day as a teen and finally quit cold turkey, only to discover it would take a decade to feel completely free of the urge to smoke. Whether it's a minor pain or a major overhaul, investing in your health is always worth it.

For your sake—and your family and employer's—do what it takes for you personally to stay in first-class physical condition. Remember, taking care of yourself is also taking care of business.

Determine your agenda for continued learning
NBJ April 2011

Our brains are amazing intelligence centers that can absorb an unlimited amount of information. So why not just download all we can?

Well, because no one is forcing us to improve ourselves. Status quo is always an option. We can listen to mind-numbing music and space out in front of the TV or we can read, network and go to school to enhance our knowledge. Personal growth has to be a conscious decision. That's your learning agenda. You either have one or you don't.

If you've made up your mind to become even more amazing, here are some tips for establishing a learning agenda.

Be honest: Start with a little self-analysis. In your limited spare time, how many hours do you spend in a zombie-like state watching sitcoms or other sometimes-entertaining-but-more-often-totally-worthless TV programs? Ask yourself exactly what you got out of all those hours. Likely your answer will be "nothing!" Find out where you're *honestly* at before you develop a personal learning agenda.

Be open: Open your mind to learning all kinds of things. The broader your knowledge base is the more interesting you are to others. Likewise, the more you know the more you will be sought after for business meetings and social events. People we meet often fall into two categories: those who are interesting and you want to meet again, or those who a make you think "what a bore." We all want to fall into the "really interesting" category.

Be specific: In the business world, your learning agenda is likely multifaceted, with initiatives in reading, networking, business conferences, and possibly classes or educational television programs. The goal in this realm is to build a learning agenda that is specific and measurable, meaning you gain knowledge crucial to your job and your growth potential in it.

Be regular: Whether it's from an old-fashioned hardcopy or an e-reader, regular reading is the backbone of building a first-class knowledge base. The more you read the better you will read. Start by reading (or scanning) key trade journals, industry-specific magazines and at least one general business magazine (Forbes, Fortune or Business Week). Pay special attention to the offbeat material, which often contains the most innovative ideas.

Be book-ish: Reading books is the most time-consuming piece of a good learning agenda, but it's also the most transformational. For example, one profound book—I*n Search of Excellence*, a study of two dozen American companies that were consistently achieving outstanding performance—helped me see a clearer path for my own company. I really believe Tractor Supply Company would not be where it is today had I not read that book.

Be planful: It is easy to procrastinate and avoid the tough learning that will do us the most good. So, make a plan and write it down. For example: In the next six months I will read three books that will help me be a better person and a better business leader. That's one 300-page book every two months or 150 pages a month or five pages a day. Not sure where to start? Find a basic business strategy book (like *Good to Great* by Jim Collins), one on self-improvement (try one about communication skills) and a general knowledge read like a biography or history book.

Leaders are always on stage!
NBJ August 2012

Business leaders are always on stage. As you interact with your team, customers, sales people, friends, family—even strangers—you send a message through everything you do and speak. People observe closely your words and actions as a leader. And most will follow your example, so make it good one.

First impression: This is important and lasting, so start things off right by dressing professionally. When in doubt, dress up one level. Set your sights on making a strong and positive impression every day on everyone you meet. Always send the message: I take pride in myself.

Simple smile: Everyone wants to be around positive, happy people. You can be that person by starting with a simple smile. When you smile, it changes your outlook, can lift your mood and instantly makes you a more approachable person. It even makes you more attractive. Like they say, smile and the world smiles with you.

Firm handshake: Bone-crushing handshakes are out, and wet dishrag handshakes communicate a lack of trust and a weak personality. Always remember that a firm handshake is a sign of strong character and personal confidence, regardless of gender. There is no gender in business.

Eye contact: This quickly communicates positive self-assuredness and demonstrates your interest in what another person is saying. Direct eye contact also keeps you focused on the person you are communicating with and minimizes distractions. "Look 'em in the eye" is the golden rule of one-to-one conversation.

Intentional listening: Listening is widely considered the most powerful communication skill—and one that we all can work on. Effective communication is directly related to the *quality* of our listening. When you listen, don't do it part way; do it intently. Despite the myriad tasks and important decisions running through your head, don't allow your mind to wander. Concentrate. Others will respect and admire you when you take time to *really* listen.

Crafted communication: Your communications skills are critical, so focus on the messages you deliver in every situation. Craft your words carefully to assure that you are giving clear, unambiguous direction. When you are in front of a group, speak professionally. Keep a good pace, but don't talk so fast that people can't follow your thoughts. Use good grammar. Be polite. Say "please" and "thank you" often. And, remember, there is no upside to using foul language.

Remember, you are on stage no matter where you are. Set the right example in and out of the workplace—in both words and deeds.

There is a great deal of truth in the old adage that "your actions speak so loudly I can't hear what you say." Your image and your actions communicate everything about you, so make sure you are sending the message you want to send.

What's your reading agenda?
2014

Continuous learning is essential to business success. We know reading is a key component of learning, so do you have a reading agenda? Never dismiss the importance of regular reading for both your total knowledge and specific business acumen.

Reading comes in so many forms. Don't overlook tried-and-true newspapers—either print or online. They are essential for keeping up with current events. If you're not current, you're often already out of the conversation and may appear lost in certain situations. You can't possibly read every paper, but you should have a reasonable plan for regular reading. Scan the front pages and inside headlines, and select a handful of daily articles that look to be the most helpful for you. Three suggestions:

- ➢ Local paper: Know the key news items and trends in your community
- ➢ Nashville Business Journal: Keep up with local businesses, competitors and leaders
- ➢ Wall Street Journal: Stay current on business trends in the world, nation and your industry

Magazines look at issues over longer time periods and often examine big-picture business and industry-specific trends. I typically scan the contents and highlight several articles that might be of interest. Two suggestions:

- ➢ Forbes or Fortune magazine: There are always articles of interest in these established national business magazines

> Trade journals: Find what's best in your industry and keep up at least monthly

Reading books takes the most time and concentration—and is also most often put off. I do my best book reading on airplanes and on vacation. I also recommend choosing new authors each time since so many second books are a repackaging of the first book. Each year, try reading at least one book from each of these categories:

> Basic business (organization, strategy, relationships, etc.) Learning is the key.
> Leadership (business, government, historical). You need to be challenged.
> Biography (business or political leader). Or anyone you admire.
> History (preferably American). It will put things in perspective.

If you have gotten this far you might be saying to yourself that all this is great, but I don't have the time. I used to say the same thing but learned that I had to *find* the time. It's amazing where it's hidden.

Remember, reading is a key to your personal growth. Knowledge is essential to your success. And finding the time is matter of personal prioritization.

Make progress with a personal learning agenda
NBJ March 2017 & Oct 2017

The world is changing faster than ever. Just 10 years ago, cell phones weren't that smart—and media wasn't very social. Now retail sales are quickly shifting from brick-and-mortar to online, while automation is reducing U.S. factory head count quicker than low-wage countries can take away the jobs. Most everything around us is changing faster than ever, which means just to keep up we have to be learning all the time.

The importance of continuous learning—especially maintaining a solid grasp of major world trends—became more acute recently while reading Johan Norberg's "Progress: 10 Reasons to Look Forward to the Future." Did you know, despite what we hear, violence worldwide is hovering near the lowest point in recorded history? There has also been huge movement toward greater freedom and equality across the globe. For starters, consider the impact these three trends may have on your professional life:

Life expectancy: Worldwide it has risen from 31 to 71 in the last 100 years and is growing all the time. Your peers are working longer, which might mean a longer path to that dream job. Or you might wind up hiring 80-year-olds—a thought that may not have crossed your mind a decade ago. How will longer lifetimes impact your particular workplace or industry?

Global literacy: Worldwide 86% of people are now literate, up from just 40% in 1950. That means the work you do may now see competition from around the globe, not just the next town over. What new competition is your profession, company or industry facing today? How will you meet those challenges in the future?

Declining poverty: In 1981, a remarkable 44% of the world's population lived in extreme poverty; today that number is less than 10%. How can your company capitalize on this positive change? What impact will this socioeconomic advancement have on the products and services your company delivers?

The importance of a learning agenda: These are just a few of macro trends that you should know about to stay current. To excel—and maybe just survive—leaders would be well served by making a proactive "learning agenda."

Mine includes reading newspapers, magazines and books; going to as many trade and educational events as I can; and, perhaps most importantly, networking with a wide variety of professionals who know more than I do.

As you build your own learning agenda, think hard about how larger cultural shifts may affect your life—and your career.

- How will the products and services you produce and provide change in the future?
- What skills do you need to develop to keep up?
- What else do you need to learn?

Here's your five-step challenge: 1) Read "Progress." 2) Examine how trends may impact you personally. 3) Craft a learning agenda. 4) Anticipate your future. 5) Prepare yourself for change.

3. CHARACTER

5 ways to walk the high road
NBJ July 2021

Some of my earliest memories are being taught to be honest, do the right thing and never lie. I think most young people grow up hearing those words—more often than we would like—but they certainly stick with us. As we grow into the more complex adult world definitions about what is right often get a little cloudy, but hopefully early lessons continue to guide us in our professional lives. Here are five ways to continue to "walk the high road."

Don't take what's not yours: It's not like poaching a handful of candy from the dime store; there are major implications for theft of all kinds in adulthood. Sadly, more than a few people put their hands in our company till and lost their jobs as a result. Some even destroyed what appeared to be promising careers. On the flipside, our company found ways to provide basic money management coaching to people that just needed some help in this area.

Stick to the facts: This applies to both verbal and written communication. In the short term it is easy to tell your boss what she wants to hear but that kind of truth-stretching might catch up to you later on. When speaking with your associates simply deliver the unvarnished truth or don't talk about the subject at all. It's even easier to exaggerate in written reports but, again, you never know when fumbling the facts may catch up to you.

Avoid gossip: With today's social media the avenues to gossip online are staring you in face all the time. You may rationalize that friends and associates will "never find out," but the fact is that nothing is secret any more. Gossiping seems perfectly innocent at first, but when it evolves into sharing confidential conversations it goes downhill quickly. Once you breach confidentiality, trust and relationships deteriorate. A simple rule of thumb is this: "If you can't keep it positive, keep quiet."

Think for yourself: In today's world, another key to "walking the high road" is to remain wary of anything that sounds too much like what you want to hear. I doubt I'm the only one to have been suckered into believing something that I "wanted" to believe and then sharing it—only to find out that it was an exaggeration or outright fabrication. My father taught me never to believe anything that sounds too good to be true, do my research and think for myself. It remains sage advice.

Stay calm in confrontation: When resolving conflict, lead with an even hand, honesty and the facts. Let's say you and a peer clearly disagree on an important issue and one or both of you spout off, maybe even by including a little character assignation. You are both upset and not talking to each other. The best solution is to take a breather, calmly write down your key points, sleep on it, review your notes and schedule another conversation the next day. You will certainly clarify the issues and may resolve the conflict altogether. Don't let issues like this fester. Quick resolution is the best resolution.

Walk the high road in everything you do. You will feel better about yourself, you will earn the respect of others and you will sleep sounder.

Respect drives more than productivity
NBJ May 2010

Respect is a value often ignored in life—and business. Many of us run at a break-neck pace without giving much thought to the lives of those around us. But the simple values of consideration, thoughtfulness and respect are essential elements to good leadership and healthy companies.

Respect works mutually. If you treat co-workers with respect, it is likely they will treat you this way in return, creating the foundation for a successful and productive relationship. However, if you treat an employee poorly, that person may still work for you, but will probably remain suspicious and may not support you when you need it most.

Here are some other business areas in which respect plays a key role:

Office communication: Rule No. 1: Keep no secrets. Keeping employees in the dark about business issues or fostering a secretive, untrustworthy work environment will only result in less productive employees who, fittingly, won't be willing to be team players. Open communication builds trust and respect among all people. The more we share the more we can trust, which ultimately encourages team members to work together in the spirit of cooperation and accomplishment.

Employee engagement: Support for any mission increases as team members know more about the task at hand. And valued, engaged team members are your most powerful assets. Ask opinions, discuss options and generally include each person as much as possible in the work plan. The greater the initial involvement, the more support and commitment the mission will receive, resulting in a better chance for success.

Verbal courtesy: Simply using "please" and "thank you" can go a long way in building respect. If someone gives you a pat on the back for a job well done, acknowledge that person by responding with a humble thank you. Likewise, if you make a mistake have the courage to say, "I messed it up" and apologize. Whether a situation is positive or negative, honest and sincere communication goes a long way in earning you greater respect.

Meetings and conference calls: Set the agenda, share it, stick to it, and you will encourage each attendee to be a productive member of the team. When you end a meeting or conference call on time, you have shown respect for everyone's time in a very simple way. However, if you allow the meeting or call to move off the agenda and run late, you have at once disrespected a group's time and undermined its efforts.

Communications devices: Blackberries, blueberries, cell phones… they all have a place in the business world. But you show respect by using these devices with discipline at appropriate times—and, respectfully, you all know what those should be. In case you forgot, it's disrespectful to use your device in a meeting, during a conference call or in the middle of a conversation with someone.

Returning correspondence: It is just good manners to return phone calls and emails promptly. If someone takes the initiative to write or call you, they deserve a response. If it is a salesperson, take the time to explain not now, later or never. A failure to respond can quickly lower other people's opinion of you.

Personal time: Effective leaders consistently show respect for each individual's personal time. No one should be on call 24 hours a day, seven days a week—and everyone should be entitled to communications-free vacations. Organizations can foster this mutual respect by clearly defining expectations regarding staffs' availability and really adhering to those standards.

Respect for each individual's time, talent and character can make a huge difference in a company's productivity as well as interpersonal relationships in and out of the office.

Leaders hold themselves accountable
NBJ September 2021

No matter what kind of organization you work in, ultimate accountability rests with leadership. Business leaders are accountable to stockholders. Educators are accountable to oversight boards. Government officials are accountable to voters. Military officials are accountable to political leaders.

Real accountability should reside in the heart and mind of each individual leader. Whether you're taking pride in a recent success in your business unit or owning your part in a screwup that cost the company, the good and the bad rest in your lap.

Don't deflect the blame: Leaders who have given poor direction or made bad decisions have an obligation to proactively acknowledge their error. If you screw up—and everyone does—those around you already know it, so pretending it didn't happen is just self-deluding. Instead, be a leader: Stand up and clearly acknowledge to all involved that you accept responsibility.

Leaders who try to ignore or transfer blame are simply losing the respect of the team. Leaders who quickly, fully and sincerely accept responsibility earn the admiration of all around them. Plus, this acknowledgement sets the stage to start fixing whatever can be corrected. It is amazing how people will jump on the "let's get it right" bandwagon when the leader follows this path.

Buck still stops at the top: When bad things happen way down the ladder in an organization the ultimate accountability still rests with senior leaders. For example, when there's a culture breakdown that yields serous dishonesty and malfeasance the buck still stops at the top. Castigating minor players for major issues shows a lack of serious accountability.

Here's one piece of advice that has really stuck with me: Communicate the most when you are in trouble. You may want nothing more than to stick your head in the sand, hoping all will go away, but the bad stuff never does. Facing it boldly is the only way forward.

When to move on: We've established that as a leader you are always accountable. But how you accept responsibility and deal with the recovery steps will be critical to your future success or failure.

Sometimes that may even mean moving on. When a leader has grossly failed, it may signal a time for change. Leaders must look in the mirror and reflect deeply on the situation. There might be an opportunity to transfer or step back. If the situation is serious enough the best decision could be resignation. And if that is the case, always take the first step—don't wait to be told you are going.

Great leaders walk the high road with total honesty about all situations and then take full responsibility for everything on their watch.

Own your successes, and your failures
September 2013

From the time I wake up each morning I know that I am 100% accountable for everything I do. I take responsibility for every action I take and every word I speak. I know there is never a right time to place blame on others for the things I do.

As a business leader, I also know that I am "on stage" all the time. Everything I do reflects on my character and reputation. Crack a good joke that makes others laugh and I'm off to a good start. Try an off-color joke and I never know who I may have offended. Sound and act look like a grouch and that is how others will see me.

I'm also accountable when I deliver a speech. If it's good, I see people paying attention, taking notes and giving feedback afterward. On the other hand, if I see eyes wandering and mouths whispering, I know I have not connected. But ultimately, this too is on my shoulders.

Acknowledging mistakes: I have screwed up many times in my long career—we all have. When I realize what I have done, however, I take personal responsibility, acting quickly to repair whatever is broken. If the problem is operational then I work to fix the mess as fast as is practical. If it is a matter of interpersonal communication that turned out badly, I work to mend the wounds as soon as possible. In most cases a simple yet sincere apology usually gets things back on track.

Over the years I have been in a position to make some pretty big decisions. The higher a leader's rank, the greater the impact of those decisions. I have made some good ones and I have made some doozies. For those missteps, it's crucial to say loudly "I screwed up," because everyone else already knows it. If you don't acknowledge the facts, you just appear a cowardly buffoon in the eyes of your team.

The same principles apply in personal life. If I messed up something with my wife, I start with an apology and work forward from there. In earlier years, I scheduled my time to attend my daughter's swim meets and my son's baseball games, and if I had to miss one, I took personal responsibility.

The point is that we are responsible for our actions—all of them—and any attempt to deny or postpone that just puts us deeper in quicksand. As leaders, no matter what we do, good or bad, we are singularly accountable.

Build your brand with smiles and a firm handshake
NBJ April 2016

You are your brand. Everything you say and do communicates your brand—your mark, identification, label, distinct characteristics—to everyone you come in contact with, so do all you can to build the strongest brand image possible for yourself. Each time you interact with others it sends a message, and you want your message to convey your ethics and essence. Here a few thoughts on building your personal brand.

Look sharp: Your appearance is the starting point. We have all heard that a first glance often becomes a lasting impression, so get it right every time. Dress for your position or, better yet, dress for the position to which you aspire. Check yourself in the mirror before you leave for work. Any doubts? Dress one level up. Not sure about appearance? Get some help from a mentor—a friend at a higher-level position or a professional coach.

Shake right: An appropriately firm handshake sends a clear signal of confidence and character. A weak handshake could imply that you are unsure of yourself. However, an overpowering handshake makes others uncomfortable and raises other questions about the authenticity of your character. A sweaty handshake might give away your nervousness in your own skin.

Make eye contact: Direct eye contact sends a message of strength. When you look down it may suggest you have something to hide. When you're constantly looking elsewhere the message you send is that you are disinterested. The right amount of eye contact conveys sincerity, interest and honesty.

Get acquainted: Make sure introductions are clear and that names and, and in most cases, job titles or responsibilities are understood. In large groups name badges are often helpful for breaking the ice and encouraging follow up. You don't want people leaving asking themselves, "Who was that person?"

Stay engaged: Don't get sidetracked. Stay in the game and concentrate. You earn respect when you listen and pay attention. Digest what is communicated, ask good questions and wait your turn to participate. Looking distracted and unfocused will only work to damage your brand, leaving people with a poor impression of you.

Trash distractions: Turn the cell phone off or, better yet, leave it somewhere else entirely. Nothing can end a meaningful interaction faster than one party stopping to answer an almost-always-less-important call. Get out from behind your desk and away from your computer so you are not even tempted to look at the latest email. If something does distract you, write a quick note, put it away and continue with business.

Smile a lot: The old expression is so true: "Smile and the world smiles with you." A smile instantly communicates warmth, confidence and character. A stern look or frown may send a message of insincerity and lack of interest; still worse, to some people it could convey deceit and dishonesty. Just think how much better you feel when talking with a person who smiles.

Your brand is everything and only you can build and shape your brand. The thoughts above are just part of your life-long brand-building mission. Be positive about all you do and diligently work to project that image to others. It is not just an image—it's you.

Professionals keep it clean
May 2014

Vulgarity doesn't belong in business. I realized this a few years back at a corporate meeting when a feisty young executive tried to convince us of his point by using some pretty rough language. While he thought his choice words were demonstrating passion, I found his delivery just plain unprofessional. In fact, the offensive language altered the whole focus of the presentation and took away from the core proposal. I wondered why he thought it necessary to use such crude content when he could have made the same point with less cussing and more creativity.

Today bad language is more common than ever in the media, on television and in the movies. It seems to be everywhere and increasingly accepted, particularly among younger generations. But the reality is plenty of people don't accept vulgarity—and using it may actually undermine your efforts. Since the natural setup of business means most "bosses" are older, and perhaps less receptive to foul language, next time you're considering some bad verbiage, take a second to ask:

- How does my boss feel about this type of language?
- Are my peers just pretending to be OK with it? Are they really laughing or cringing?
- Who's in the room and what are their true thoughts on the subject?
- And, of course, when in doubt, ask, "What would my mom say?"

You may think you know the answers to these questions, but you may not. And not knowing puts you in an awkward position. Additionally, you may think choice words add to your persuasiveness, but many people are simply turned off by uncouth language and won't even take the time to consider what you have to say.

There is no upside to using vulgarity and you may be offending others. It could affect your reputation, your effectiveness in business and even your next promotion. Bottom line: There's simply no logical reason to use foul language—and a lot of career risk if you do. Winners keep it clean.

Settle down: learn to control your emotions
NBJ June 2015

We all get emotional and wound up from time to time about one topic or another. But leaders, who are always "on stage" and therefore always setting an example, have to control these emotions in each and every situation. Why? Because when you lose it, you also risk losing the respect of your people. If an employee sees you blow up, the likelihood of maintaining constructive communication diminishes. It's hard to count on honest, accurate feedback when your boss is volatile.

If you feel emotion building and think there's some possibility that you will express your anger in a detrimental way, use your "fuse" to trigger a two-step cool down: First, take a deep breath. Then excuse yourself. Go someplace (the break room, your car, a nearby park) or do something (squeeze a therapy ball, put on some music, write down your thoughts) that will help you start to gain control over your emotions.

After struggling to curb my own temper when I was younger, I learned a trick that helped me to back off and simmer down. My cool-down exercise was always to walk outside in some fresh air for some fresh perspective. A stroll down the street or around the block seemed to give me just enough time to bring things back to earth. While all humans have emotions and we would never want to pretend that we're super-human, strong leaders can use simple tools like these to ensure emotions don't get the upper hand.

In some cases, leaders must deal with emotional outbursts from their own bosses, which presents another type of challenge. In this case my advice remains the same: Keep yourself cool, and don't let your boss's emotions feed your emotions. Stick to the facts and try to postpone a heated conversation to a later date.

Another helpful practice is to ask the advice of a trusted friend or family member outside of your company. Friends often ask questions that you have not considered and they may help you think in different ways. With one particular emotional situation during my professional career, I turned to my wife for outside perspective. She asked a series of what at the time seemed like odd inquiries, but ultimately, they led me to a unique and very effective approach to dealing with the difficult situation.

No one is immune to experiencing emotion in the workplace. How often have you gotten an email that fires you up and you say to yourself, "I am going to straighten out that jerk!" Fine. Draft your firebrand response, read it over and then immediately put it in your draft file. Do not send it. Sleep on it. The next morning you will modify your response, mellow it or ideally not send it at all. Time has a way of taking the raw emotion out of communication, and the best remedy is usually a calm, well-planned face-to-face talk or telephone call a day or two later.

No matter what your role, don't let your emotions take control. Figure out some internal mechanisms that work best for you—and start using them to take charge of yourself.

Dump the negativity: positive leadership builds confidence, creates winning teams
NBJ August 2014; (Orig. Positive leaders are winners)

We all know that "bad" news sells. We hear a continuous barrage of negative stories—on television, in the papers and on the Internet. When leaders repeat this bad news, employees tend to follow.

So why not counteract that negativity? I've found that really high-class leaders know how to focus on positive topics with generally top-notch results. Here are a few positive facts about our world today:

- ➢ Poverty and starvation are at the lowest levels in recorded history
- ➢ Worldwide violence is at the lowest level in history
- ➢ U.S. crime rates have been on a downward spiral for more than 30 years

> Global literacy is at the highest level ever
> More people live in democratic countries than any time in history

The reality is we live in an ever-improving world, and as leaders we need to talk about the good things taking place around us. People react positively to positive thoughts and actions, so just think about the influence you can have on your team when you share optimistically.

The importance of everyday actions: It's just as important to be positive in your actions as a leader.

> If you micro-manage you are throwing a big wet blanket over the initiative of your team.
> If you criticize in front of others, you are demoralizing and losing respect at the same time.
> If you lose your cool you are losing your position with your people.
> If you are not patting folks on the back for a good job you are missing an opportunity to build confidence and teamwork.

Take some time evaluate your leadership practices. I hope you can truly say that you are a positive leader.

Great leaders also encourage optimistic team thinking by emphasizing what really counts, regardless of day-to-day pressures. You will get the best ideas and the strongest performance by being positively engaged and inclusive. You will get the least participation and the poorest productivity when you are critical and negative. When the boss is future-focused, looking for the good in everything, teams bond and can achieve greater success. Plus, statistics show positive people live longer!

Here are a few ways you can work toward being a more positive leader:

- ➢ Have a clear long-term plan for your business unit. Share it regularly with your team.
- ➢ Recognize good performance with a pat on the back, at least daily.
- ➢ Celebrate accomplishment as frequently as it happens.
- ➢ Give regular, detailed performance feedback to everyone on your team.
- ➢ Share everything—keep no secrets.

Employees thrive under positive leadership. Assess your performance, build your plan, be positive every day and watch the astonishing results.

Need a change? Leave the bad attitude at home
NBJ July 2015 (Orig. Pitch in! Be Positive!)

In our culture we tend to share the bad and keep the good to ourselves. Unfortunately, the practice plays out in the workplace, too. People criticize the company and grumble about the boss. What if we were to turn that practice upside-down? It's my experience that positive, enthusiastic attitudes are the key to moving organizations in the right direction.

But like anyone else, I had to learn this the hard way. A seasoned businessman who was new to retail replaced my boss, the company president, shortly after I joined Tractor Supply. Since we all liked the previous president, it was natural to resent the new guy. But I soon realized that complaining about the change was never going to help the situation. So, I decided to work closely with our new president while many of my peers kept their distance. I gained newfound confidence by passing on my retail knowledge to the new boss. In return, he helped me grow and mature as a leader.

My hard work and support of the new boss paid off handsomely several months later when he promoted me to Senior VP, the No. 2 position in the company. The lesson? I achieved this outcome simply by changing my attitude from negative to positive—and pitching in. I was in the right place at the right time, and took advantage of the opportunity. Looking back, I realize that these early actions put me on the path to becoming president and later CEO of Tractor Supply.

Now consider your own situation. How positive are you day in and day out? We all have bad days when we get out of bed on wrong side, but that needs to stay at the bedside and never make it to the workplace. What if we all committed to showing up for work with a positive attitude? Imagine how much better your boss could lead and how much more your team could accomplish if everyone was on the same page with an optimistic, constructive attitude. Instead of "We'll never get this done," leaders need to hear "We can."

The empowering thing is positivity and pitching in and it is all up to you. You don't have to project a loser's image, losing the respect of your peers and most likely the next promotion. Take it as a challenge to change the culture: Try to become the most enthusiastic person on your team. You might be surprised at how much respect you'll gain—and how much fun you'll have earning it.

Can you stay cool?
NBJ May 2013

Controlling your emotions is a crucial leadership skill. When you lead other people, situations can quickly become tense and prompt you to say things in the moment that you may regret later.

I'll never forget one incident that drove this point home more than any other in my career. Working in a high-stress environment, I got on an employee's case about a trivial matter. He exploded at me. Even though he was the one who lost it, I knew I was off base for provoking the argument. I recognized my insensitivity to the substantial stress he was under at the time.

Before the day was over, I went to his work area with a sincere apology. We patched things up and were soon back to a normal business relationship. Looking back, I realize that a little common sense and compassion on my side would have avoided the whole situation.

The point is, it's not easy to stay cool in the everyday mix of fast-paced business. And if you are a Type A personality that likes to control the environment, it's even harder. We've all had those times when we lose it, blowing a fuse at a peer, team member or even the boss.

Coping mechanisms: The obvious way to avoid these situations is to use self-control. But that's often easier said than done. Here are some ways to begin instituting more everyday restraint:

> **Be quiet:** When you feel emotions getting to you in a tense business setting, start to recognize this feeling and discipline yourself to be silent. Take a deep breath and tell yourself to, well, just "shut up."
>
> **Target triggers:** After a heated event or throughout a typical day, try to analyze what triggers your emotions. Maybe even write them down. You'll start to put in place internal trip switches to control these reactions before they reach critical mass.
>
> **Walk away:** My personal cure for highly emotional situations is to be quiet, excuse myself and walk away. Like a "time out" for young children, a walk outside in the fresh air works wonders. Take the opportunity to cool down, think more rationally about the situation and consider ways that you could conduct yourself more appropriately.
>
> **Face it:** The same day, try to return to the topic that created the conflict. Avoiding touchy situations often causes underlying tension, which could very well lead to more long-term difficulty than the original issue. The quicker you patch

things up, the less pain there is on both sides and the sooner things can return to normal.

Really good leaders find creative ways to stay cool even in the most stressful times. How cool are you?

Take time to think
NBJ March 2013

It's amazing how little independent, critical thinking we do these days. We seldom set aside time to really contemplate our lives and our future with a long-term perspective.

Most of us tear through life at a breakneck pace. We're distracted from morning until night with devices, and we rely so much on the Internet, social media and other people's opinions to inform our thinking. What if we turned it all off for a few moments?

Hear that? It's quiet. Just how I like it. For decades, I've climbed into my car, leaving all distractions and diversions behind, in order to do my serious, in-depth thinking. Usually this leads me to the quiet upper level of a parking garage. It's nothing fancy, but it works.

Be sure to bring a pen and paper to write your thoughts. Turn everything off. Then close your eyes and steady your thoughts. The goal is to think about serious leadership topics with an eye to your long-term future. I suggest breaking your thinking into three different topics: your current position, future career and personal life.

First, think about your current role and ask yourself some serious questions like:

> How would I evaluate the performance of my business unit?
> How is my team performing?
> What am I doing to help my people be successful?
> Do I have a backup plan if someone gets promoted, transfers or leaves?

> What plans do I have for my operation in six months, a year and two years from now?
>
> Have I put in place all the components for long-term success?

The bottom line is to make s clear assessment of your organization's performance. Then start to put in place whatever changes are needed to achieve maximum success.

Second, think about your career, and ask yourself questions like these:

> Being totally honest, how is my performance?
> What plans do I have to improve?
> Where do I want to be a year from now? Two years from now?
> Do I have career development plan?
> Have I discussed a plan with my boss?
> Have I enrolled in the necessary courses?
> Am I attending the trade shows, networking events, webinars, etc. that will lead to my development?

The point of this thinking is to identify areas of improvement, as well as resources that you can use to get to where you want to be. Use your boss as an advisor. Sign up for a class. Write down five things you want to achieve by the end of the year.

Third, think about your personal life—family and friends—and ask:

> How am I doing overall?
> Am I spending time with the kids?
> Did I take my spouse out to dinner last month?
> Did we plan our vacation ahead of time?
> Have I talked to my best friend this week?
> Have I told those who are closest to me that I love them?
> Do I need to alter my behavior?

The key to this one—and all of these topics—is to be honest. It's OK. You're alone. No one knows. Start to think about how the balance of your professional and personal life can increase your overall happiness and make you a stronger, more dynamic leader.

I do this kind of serious thinking several times a year and often make some serious, long-term alterations in my life. If you really devote time to dedicated quiet thinking, I can just about guarantee you'll make some positive changes in your life.

4. COMMUNICATION

The secret of great leaders: learn to communicate well
Nashville Business Journal—September 2010

What do the world's best leaders consider their secret to success? Communication. There's no limit to the number of skills a good leader must possess, but in order to become a truly *effective* leader you have to be really good at communicating with the people in your life. Here are some ways to develop communication skills:

Be a great conversationalist: Engage in meaningful conversation at every possible opportunity. Be prepared with several good questions for every occasion. And when you ask questions be sure to listen carefully. You will gain respect when you listen more than you talk. Stay up on current events so you converse intelligently, but don't allow yourself to get pulled in emotionally by discussions about religion, politics and gossip.

Prepare for business and social events: Prior to attending any business or social event, learn all you can about the event and the participants. Prepare a list of key people you plan to meet and be prepared to engage each person in meaningful conversation. Also be prepared to move away politely from conversations that are not of interest. Leaders earn the respect of others with substantial and engaged discussions.

Say it in person: When it comes to having a tough conversation, plan your thoughts carefully and handle it face to face. If you can't meet in person, use the phone. Don't try to resolve an important and/or difficult issue in a written letter or over email.

Sleep on it: When your blood begins to boil over the content of an email or the tone of a conversation, take a deep breath, count to 10 and try to relax. An emotional response can get you in trouble quickly, so refrain from responding in the heat of the moment. Just sleep on it. Your response the following day, if you respond at all, will be more clear, rational and professional.

Write effectively: With digital communication—text and email messaging—the norm these days, it is even more important to hone your written skills. From time to time in your leadership role you will also write business letters and prepare reports. Unfortunately, there are situations where leaders can't move above a certain level because of their inability to write (and therefore communicate) effectively. Don't hesitate to enlist the aid of a friend to polish important written materials. And, as with any skill, practice is the key. The more you write the better you will write.

Speak in public: If you are going to be a true leader you have to be able to speak effectively to the people you are leading. It's your job to set the goals, explain the mission and then motivate your team to make it all happen. However, for some, public speaking is terrifying. If you're one of these people, tackle that fear. Start by planning ahead: Know your audience and materials; outline (general thoughts, not word for word) your speech; recite opening and closing lines; and then practice by speaking out loud or training with an audio/video recording. Once you're more comfortable, speak frequently. Seize every opportunity to practice your new skill.

Remember, becoming a good communicator is a life-long journey. It doesn't happen overnight. Work on honing your communication skills—interpersonal conversations, writing and public speaking—each day and you will build a foundation for becoming a stronger and more confident leader.

Communicating in today's world
NBJ November 2013

Technology is moving forward at a breakneck pace—and the world of communication is changing just as fast. Leaders in the business world need to know how to balance both technology-enhanced and traditional communication tools. Here are a few simple tips:

Text: Texting in the business sphere is best kept to messages that relay short facts or scheduling information, such as letting an employee know you are stuck in traffic and will be five minutes late to a lunch meeting, or asking a team member to bring a particular document to an out-of-office conference.

Email: Email is the most routine way we conduct business today. But remember, people are busy, get overloaded with emails and often scan content, so keep emails succinct and use bullet points for items you need others to grasp quickly. Like most CEOs, I simply deleted any email longer than one page. Also avoid overusing pictures, graphics or other unnecessary attachments. Most importantly, don't vent in an email. If you are upset about a subject, sit on your email overnight and you'll most likely tone it down or delete it by the next morning.

Facebook: As a social tool that can blur the lines between personal and professional, sometimes getting even well-intentioned leaders in hot water, it's best to steer clear of Facebook for business communication. Let the experts handle your company's profile and corporate communications online. Want to network digitally? Stick to LinkedIn.

E-cards & e-vites: These are casual digital communication tools, which unless designed and delivered very thoughtfully, are often overlooked or even deleted by recipients. For important or official business communication, revert to traditional paper cards and invitations. Not only does paper require people to stop while they physically open material, it can convey a classier, more professional tone.

Cell phone: When you are in a one-on-one meeting with a team member, conducting a business lunch or discussing details in the boardroom, the only acceptable thing to do is turn off your cell phone. All the way off. While it may seem hard to unplug completely when you feel like you might miss important developments, the truth is you might be missing important interpersonal communication that could affect productivity just as much.

Telephone: Ah, how we've forgotten the good ole' horn. With email and text taking over the world, we've nearly eliminated the need to talk on the telephone or in person. However, we haven't eliminated the *meaning* behind non-digital communication. When a topic is really important or might get misconstrued through email, pick up the phone. Better yet, go see the person face to face.

Pen & paper: Put your most important communication in writing that's well organized and easy to read. Your work will be taken more seriously if you can write professionally, accurately and concisely. If you need help in this area, get some input from an associate who really knows how to put thoughts in writing. When in doubt, go old-fashioned. You'll make a lasting impression.

Trust, transparency is the foundation of leadership
NBJ March 2019

Good supervisors demonstrate daily that they can be counted on for help and advice. Showing that kind of support leads directly to a culture of trust—from leader to learner—and often translates to a better peer-to-peer working environment as well.

In fact, trust among a team can mean the difference between a successful leader and one who struggles along but always wonders why. When the people you're paid to guide believe in you and trust what you say, your odds of success skyrocket. The opposite also holds true: If your team does not trust you, your success will also have limits.

Confident leaders know that it takes hard work to build a trusting environment in which all players work well together. But it's worth it. Here are a few ways to start nurturing the best possible atmosphere at work.

Be honest and transparent in all dealings: Treat every team member with the same degree of respect that you expect for yourself. Unfortunately, one boss I had demonstrated a style that didn't work—only sharing on what he deemed a "need to know" basis. Holding back or changing the rules too often is a quick path to losing the commitment of your people.

Commit to being a no-secrets leader: My predecessor frequently reiterated that Tractor Supply was a "no-secrets" company. It was a simple yet powerful statement because it opened up for discussion every important topic. Transparency is the path to understanding and being open can lead to fresh problem-solving and operational improvements. Consider letting your people know that you are unequivocally a no-secrets leader.

Share your plans and goals with your team: When your employees know which direction you are heading, they are best positioned to get you across the goal line. Share your mission and your values so people know the real "you." This will help build authentic bonds that yield the greatest successes. Even if you are a private person by nature, work toward an attitude of sharing everything.

Keep operating standards consistent: That means all parties should have logical, clearly understandable day-to-day directions. Baseball players need to know that the strike zone never changes. Employees need to understand measures of performance and be able to judge their own productivity. Operating standards should contain no after-the-fact surprises.

Become a listening expert: In a fast-paced world, leaders need to discipline themselves to take the time to really listen to employees. Ask probing questions on important topics. Remember that sometimes the real message may be under the surface. And if you receive feedback you don't like, the first response should always be "thank you." If you're always on the defensive that may be last time you receive honest feedback.

Recognize every success: Wise words from my former mentor: "Recognition is the No. 1 motivator." A thoughtful pat on the back goes further than you realize. Celebrate every success, even small ones, in whatever way makes the most sense in your professional environment.

Teach and coach: Do everything you can to help your people build skills and become more productive. Teaching will earn the lasting respect and admiration of your employees. I'll bet when you are old and gray you will take more pride in the human talent you helped develop than in any other single business accomplishment.

Building trust in your team is the foundation of leadership success. When your people understand you and believe in you, they will work with you to help achieve your goals. So, put aside some time to build a strategy for developing trust in your organization. It will pay off.

Want to maximize results? Learn to keep it simple
NBJ June 2019

Ask what time it is and sometimes you'll hear about how to build a watch. While even the most effective leaders try to keep things simple, in many instances that's not so easy. It's very common to get so wrapped up in our work that we over-explain because we are passionate about what we do. But it is up to us as leaders to keep communication flowing with just the right amount of detail.

Putting it in writing: Think of a written presentation as a business advertisement for your idea. The goal is to peak interest and then respond if the boss wants more detailed information. Most leaders will skim through or in some cases not even read long detailed paragraphs. So, keep it concise: Don't write more than you need. A few opening sentences followed by a half dozen or so headlined bullet points will go a long way to sell your thoughts.

Selling your idea: When you make your pitch to senior leaders remember that they generally don't want to hear about the details; they want to know about the big picture. For example, a big-picture real estate plan might sound like this: "The proposal is to open a 20,000-square-foot store in Springfield at the intersection of Routes 1 and 2. The cost will be $1 million and the construction will be completed by September 1." If the plan is well received, only then is it time to drill down into details that leaders need to make a decision.

Measuring performance: All employees want to know how they're doing on the job. So, design performance measures so they're clear, readily available and easy to understand. Also, make sure your people know the criteria for measuring performance and hear from you regularly about progress. In retail, for example, the most important measure is sales. So, report it daily and directly.

Setting direction: The people on your team can only carry out a mission if they can clearly understand it. Ten operational goals won't cut it. It's impossible to focus effectively on so many objectives. So, limit your direction to two or three key goals for your organization. Then repeat those simplified directives. Repetition will increase focus on the few big-picture topics that are really important.

Taking charge: If you are in one of those meetings where the inundation of detail has obscured the big picture, speak up. If you are leading the meeting, quickly move the agenda back to the big picture. If not, ask for a short break to speak with the leader. When participants are overwhelmed with minutiae nothing with get accomplished. So, take charge of the situation.

Dealing with techy types: Some leaders in the tech world are excellent communicators and some tend to devolve into details that are hard for others to comprehend. Our role as leaders is to recognize these situations and then coach our tech people in the most effective ways to translate and sell their important ideas.

Teaching simplicity: Both in writing and speech, coach your people to put everything in terms that are easy to understand. Sometimes you will have to help team members cut out excess sentences and unnecessary words in written materials. When communicating verbally, you may have to guide them get to the point faster. When you detect too much detail, it's time to put on your coaching hat.

Leaders who preach simplicity in everything often get the best results. Why? At the most elemental level, when teams are not bogged down with excessive data, organizations can accomplish more. So, make simplicity a core topic of your leadership discussions. And watch others follow your lead.

Dive into public speaking
NBJ October 2012

One of the most common fears in life is speaking in public.

I have seen people of all ages freeze when put in front of a group to deliver a talk. Being videotaped—and having your words permanently recorded—adds yet another element of stress to public speaking. We have all been there. And must go there again.

If you are on a leadership path you will have to deliver speeches from time to time, so you are going to have to get used to it. In fact, solid public speaking often separates the big stars from the small ones.

Make up your mind now to speak publicly, whether to a small or large group, as often as possible. Like any other skill in life, your public speaking will improve simply by doing it more regularly. While the old adage "practice makes perfect" may not fully apply here, the more you talk in public the smoother you will speak and the less anxiety you will have about it.

Here are few tips for a painless public speech:

- **Stay in bounds:** Stick to topics on which you are knowledgeable and confident. Avoid speaking on new topics, which will add a new level of anxiety to your speaking engagement.
- **Plan ahead:** Start working on a plan for your talk as early as possible. The more comfortable you are with your subject matter, the less stress you will feel on the big day.
- **Big bullets:** Outline your talk with bullet points, using short phrases. You can speak more naturally and conversationally from an outline. Don't try to memorize your talk; you will stumble and mistakes will appear more obvious.
- **Opening lines:** Get your first few sentences down pat. A strong leading thought that's delivered well builds confidence and sets the tone.
- **Talk to yourself:** Practice out loud in front of a mirror. Record your speech and listen to it. Video is even better. It's the best training tool for seeing all of your physical movements, hear-

- **Prep time:** Get to your stage early and learn about your surroundings and the people in the space. Make sure you are comfortable with the podium, microphone, lighting, etc., so there will be no surprises.
- **Step outside yourself:** While we may perspire a bit and our hearts may race, much of our nervousness is emotional and isn't noticeable externally.
- **Move on:** Miss a point in your talk? Keep going. No one in the audience knows.
- **Confident close:** A closing statement that drives home key takeaways is critical. Prepare a clear close so you can end smoothly and confidently.

Now stop procrastinating and go write a speech. The sooner you start, the sooner you will become a more confident speaker.

How to make good first impressions
NBJ November 2015

First impressions are everything in life and in business, so be sure to make good ones. Think about people you have met over the years. You might find that you immediately picture the first moment you met—that initial impression. And that impression is difficult to change, so make every inaugural meeting work in your favor, not against you or your business.

The receptionist: This is one of the first visual points of contact in the business world so strive to make it work to your company's benefit. Isn't a chipper, well-dressed, helpful, conversational professional who we all want to greet us? This first contact sends a critical message about your organization. Make it a positive one.

The salesperson: This is another first point of contact with potentially large financial implications. In this case each element must be correct at the outset—professional appearance, solid handshake, a smile and direct eye contact. When these basics begin right then subsequent conversation about a product and service has a much better chance of success.

The "switchboard:" In this situation we have two options: machine (common) or human (preferred). If using an answering machine, make sure your recorded message is crisp, friendly and gets to the point quickly, without too many confusing options. You goal is to make it easy and efficient for the caller to connect with the party they are looking for. If you can staff folks to answer the phone that's even better. Train them to use a warm and friendly tone to make callers glad they called. For example, "Hello this is Joe Scarlett. Thank you for calling the Scarlett Widget Company today. How may I help you?"

The voicemail: This is another wildly varying point of first contact, from the anonymous, automated "leave a message at the tone" version, to my all-time favorite "personalized with passion" voicemail style, which I've found great success with over the years. My version is updated weekly and includes key information, plus a status update. Example: "Hello this is Joe Scarlett. Thanks for calling. I'm on the road this week visiting stores in Nebraska, back in the office on Friday. Leave me a message and I will get back to you Friday—or maybe even today." A quality voicemail leaves the caller feeling informed and a little warm-and-fuzzy about you.

First impressions can make all the difference in the world. Make sure that yours are first class.

Conversation skills are a must
NBJ 9/4/15

Knowing how to carry on an effective conversation is essential to building your business network. This can be very challenging for some leaders who tend to be shy in social situations. But the best way to overcome any fear is to face it, over and over. Eventually you will become desensitized to the anxiety.

So, to become a good conversationalist, you've got to show up regularly and come prepared. You might be surprised at how quickly the respect you build by taking the initiative to learn to converse effectively can overcome what you thought was shyness. I had to learn this myself. I used to be very timid when speaking in front of a group, but I knew that I had to master this essential skill if I was to become a successful business leader. I had to force myself into those situations, and over time I developed confidence. Now I regularly speak in front of the public.

Here are some other tips to help you become a stronger communicator:

1. **Develop a handful of questions—conversation starters—that you can use in any situation:** "How is your business going?" is a good one since most people like to boast about successes. In more social situations, "How is your family?" will quickly elicit conversation—maybe lengthier than you wanted. The point is to keep a few go-to questions in your pocket.
2. **Listen carefully and ask good questions:** Stay focused on what a person is saying—don't let your eyes or your mind wander. If you're engaged in a real conversation, it's easy to drill down further on the subject by asking follow-up questions. Plus, it's always better to spend more time on one topic than bounce from one topic to another. One more reminder that may sound counterintuitive: People like to talk about themselves; so, the better your questioning skills are the more people will remember *you*.
3. **Show up prepared:** When you are going to a meeting or event, make sure you study up on the subject so you can speak with confidence when some asks you a question. In addition, consider each event a learning opportunity and bring some questions about what you would like to learn most. I like to review agendas and attendance lists ahead of time. This helps me decide what topics might be of interest and whom I'd like to meet with so I can get the most out of an industry event.

Communication is the most essential leadership skill, and basic conversation is the root of verbal communication. Like all other skills in life, the more you practice the better you will perform in this area. To some degree, your success is always predicated on how others see you—so continue to polish those communication skills!

In sales it's never maybe
NBJ December 2010 (Orig. Lessons from an executive turned salesman)

In sales "no" is *way* better than maybe. I learned this lesson quickly when, after 40 years in management and executive roles at two retail companies, I became a salesman for my own executive training program through the Scarlett Leadership Institute at Belmont University.

After meeting with small groups of CEOs and listening to what skills they wanted their upcoming leaders to have, we created the Signature Executive Program. Our mission was to positively influence the quality of business leadership in Middle Tennessee by building the skills of high-potential, upwardly mobile business leaders. An easy sell, right?

Selling strategies: At first it was. With a built-in customer base of 35 CEOs who helped shape the initial program it wasn't difficult to get the first class off the ground. However, we soon realized that growth requires a strong, sustained sales effort—and thick skin.

Despite knowing our target audience, easily connecting with the right people and understanding the salesperson's proven success model—fulfilling every customer's needs accurately, quickly and with a smile—I quickly realized that the buyer still has all the power.

In my previous job I was in the pole position. I led people, built teams, set direction and held my direct reports accountable—typical executive responsibilities. Now, as a salesperson, I was on the other side.

Response earns respect: My transition from executive to part-time salesman was interesting, enlightening and often frustrating. I worked diligently to fill classes, making scores of calls and then waiting for decisions and return calls.

I learned that sales people are not always treated with the courtesy and respect that one would expect in business. Often, I got responses like "We are studying your proposal and will get back to you." Sometimes I would hear back and other times there was simply no response at all.

My biggest lesson in this new role was a simple but profound one: What salespeople most need is a clear response. So, my request, advice, recommendation (plea if you will) on behalf of salespeople everywhere is, quite simply, to respond to us. Don't ignore us. Return calls. Even a straightforward "no" is better than nothing at all. When you respond you earn a salesperson's respect—and you help that person move on to the next task. After all, our time is just as valuable as yours, right?

Leaders: a positive attitude helps you win
NBJ February 2018 (orig: How positivity helps leaders win)

Want to win in your leadership role? Keep it positive. While it can be a challenge, some of the most memorable leaders have demonstrated a persistently positive and enthusiastic attitude. The capacity to show positivity day in and day out is not only a benchmark of true leadership, but can also set the tone for others to achieve the same.

What does a positive attitude look like?

- Be optimistic about the future—take a "we can do it" approach to every challenge
- Pat people on the back for a job well done and do it regularly
- Share success stories about outstanding individual and team performances
- Celebrate big—and sometimes not-so-big—victories
- Communicate with everyone around you in a confident, encouraging way
- See every day as a sunny one—don't allow anything or anyone to rain on your parade

We all know how it feels to be positive, and we have also encountered negative people who always look on the dark side. Who would you choose to be around? The answer is obvious. As a leader, your behavior sets the tone for your team and often other employees that you may not even know. Don't underestimate the impact your positive attitude can have on others—at work and at home.

Why is it important for leaders to have a positive attitude?

- Productivity is higher in motivated, enthusiastic teams
- Errors are measurably lower in high-morale work units
- New ideas flow freely from engaged workers
- Employees working in positive work climates have measurably lower turnover
- Inspired teams produce future leaders and innovators

When your business unit is cohesive, working together in a positive and constructive environment, results will simply be much better. But the magic doesn't happen spontaneously. It all begins with a leader who starts the workday looking on the bright side—and who can sustain that attitude all day long.

Staying positive, however, doesn't mean you avoid or downplay serious issues. It just means you can confront those difficult circumstances from a more positive place. In fact, once you've established an environment of high morale and everyone's invested in maintaining a happy, healthy culture, you might be able to resolve workplace issues quicker than ever before.

How will a positive attitude help your career and personal life?

- Your team will work harder, communicate better and engage more
- Your peers will be more apt to partner with you on daily work and especially on special projects
- You'll earn respect (and plenty of new friends) by keeping a good attitude about life

➤ You'll earn points with the boss by being that upbeat and positive person he or she can count on
➤ A positive attitude of gratitude will attract further happiness in your life, according to studies
➤ Family relationships will grow stronger when built on an upbeat, positive foundation
➤ You might just extend your life! Positive people actually live longer when compared to those with poor attitudes

So, psych yourself up, carve out that motivating "me time" and start some positivity practices. It will pay off for you in more ways than you can count. You want to advance your career. Everyone wants to work with a happy leader. Don't let them—or yourself—down!

5. LEADERSHIP

Simple rules for being the best leader you can be
Nashville Business Journal March 2010

True leaders are transparent. They earn respect with clear, open and honest communication. And they build a respectful environment by demonstrating personal integrity, taking a genuine interest in employees and their work, and trusting enough to delegate when necessary.

Be a model—at all times: As a leader you are always on stage. Your actions and words directly impact those around you and influence the results of your business unit. Your team sees every move and listens to each word, so it's up to you to model the performance you expect from them. Attitude is contagious. If we want our team to have an outstanding outlook, we must first set the example by personally demonstrating the positive and enthusiastic attitude we expect from them.

Keep no secrets: One of my mentors was as a proponent of being a "no secrets" leader. He made the point that there is no advantage to keeping secrets—and there is tremendous benefit to sharing all that you know. Sharing knowledge is personally liberating and also empowering for those around you. Ultimately, it builds respect for you as a leader.

Set clear direction: The people that work for you simply want realistic expectations and straightforward direction to perform their work. If you want them to get the job done well, be clear and consistent up front, measure results along the way and give constructive performance feedback when the job is done. Then, when someone does a good job, don't waste time handing out a hearty pat on the back.

Remove obstacles: A leader's role is to clear potential roadblocks out of the way so that our people can be outstanding performers. It is particularly important that people on the "frontline" have the support they need to achieve maximum results. We win in business when our team exceeds performance expectations, so we need to ensure that they have a clear path to success: the best information and tools available to perform effectively.

Wear your coach's cap: Take the time to teach each member of your team the skills required to be an outstanding performer. There is no greater reward than coaching someone and then standing back to watch that person achieve beyond their expectations. Coaching that develops both individual and team skills will, in turn, build your stature in their eyes as the true leader of the team.

Trust and delegate: Trust is an essential component of leadership. It's the key to moving from task manager to inspirational leader. But it's also one of the most difficult growth hurdles that young executives face: to delegate and then trust others to do what the boss still thinks he can do better. Most importantly, we must trust to earn trust. Our people will trust us when we clearly communicate the goals and objectives of our business unit—and then empower the team to get the job done.

The big secret about leadership is that there are no secrets. Leadership is comprised of a liberal application of common sense coupled with a little compassion and a lot of enthusiasm.

Successful leaders anticipate the future
NBJ October 2013

What's the one thing great business leaders of the last century have seen more clearly than the average person? The future. These innovators may not have fully grasped the long-term impact of their initiatives at the time, but their forward-looking, breakthrough ideas have changed the world. And in that is a lesson for all of us.

For example, when his competitors were focused on big, heavy and expensive vehicles, Henry Ford saw a need for a practical, low-priced automobile that would appeal to the masses. His vision led to the production of more than 15 million Ford Model Ts that forever changed the way Americans live and travel. His foresight also led to the introduction of assembly line manufacturing, which greatly reduced the cost of cars and most other manufactured goods, improving lives around the world.

The Wright Brothers showed us that we could defy gravity and fly, which opened a whole new means of transportation. They may not have envisioned commercial and military flight as we know it today, but the duo's creativity moved society forward in a most dramatic way.

Like all retail leaders, Sam Walton instinctively knew hard-working folks wanted lower prices, but he took steps to make affordability come to life. He led the charge of applying modern technology and advanced business practices to the retail process, which yielded revolutionary changes in one of our largest industries. The "Wal-Mart effect" has significantly driven down prices of nearly all consumer goods, benefiting people all over the world.

Steve Jobs' instincts about human nature and his grasp of technology led him down a path of rapid product innovation that revolutionized how we communicate. Just consider for a moment how smartphones and tablets have changed our lives. Today these products directly and indirectly impact almost every person on the planet.

Likewise, Larry Page and Sergey Brin knew that Internet search was a huge opportunity for technology growth, so they started on a new and different path. It's doubtful that when these two young men started, they had any idea where Google would be today. But they had an idea for a new tomorrow.

Now ask yourself what you see in the future. Are you anticipating the next events in your industry? In your company? These innovators thought differently than their contemporaries and achieved huge success. We can't all be Henry Ford or Steve Jobs, but we can begin to think boldly about the future. What breakthrough ideas do you have for your business? What innovative thoughts are rattling around in your brain? You just might have a nugget of brilliance that could make a difference.

Professionals set the tone
NBJ May 2014 (Orig. Leaders set the tone)

As a leader you have a professional and moral obligation to set the guiding tone for your team. When the workplace is full of confusion and conflict it creates a toxic environment in which people have difficulty concentrating and producing. In fact, a recent survey indicated that more than 25 percent of employee turnover is directly related to a lack of civility in the workplace.

So, remember my favorite saying: Leaders are always "on stage," setting performance and behavior standards for the team. If you use poor language, you can't criticize others for doing the same. On the other hand, if you are pleasant and cooperative and talk positively about the mission and values of the organization you will build commitment, earn respect and quickly see that others will follow suit. Here are a few ways you can start setting a better tone:

1. **Stay upbeat and connected:** Start the day with a pleasant "good morning." Then walk the floor during the day, communicating with your team about whatever topics need to be addressed. Stay plugged in to what is going on in your business. An enthusiastic pat on the back at the end of the day will do wonders for morale.
2. **Keep meetings on target and on time:** As leaders we are the ones who define the environment. When running a meeting, set a positive tone by showing up early and wrapping up on time. Respect that your employees have important work to do. Meetings are also a perfect opportunity to publicly recognize someone for a specific accomplishment.
3. **Head off unnecessary conflict:** As the leader, ultimately, you are accountable for your team's actions. While there is a fine line between sticking your nose in and letting employees sort out conflicts, time and experience will help you better understand when to stand up and when to observe from afar. In some situations, you may just need to be the moderator while both sides vent.

When all is said and done, the leader's example is the most important influence in the workplace. Communicate clearly on both major and minor topics, and don't procrastinate about serious issues that could snowball. Lead with a compassionate and constructive tone, and in return you will earn maximum respect and results.

Leaders maintain perspective by creating a clear focus
NBJ June 1, 2018

One of the things new managers wrestle with most is finding a clear sense of focus. It's easy to get involved in tedious tasks and take on more projects than you can handle. Inevitably that leads to getting lost in the weeds, and dragging your team through the muck.

Things get even more muddled when the whole company loses track of the big picture. In an environment of inconsistency and constant change comes conflict and confusion for employees at all levels, which can cause an organization to implode.

The top establishments attract and nurture leaders who know how to maintain perspective with clear, consistent focus. For example, in a retail business like Tractor Supply, where happy customers lead to healthy sales, we know that the principles of good customer service will always drive sales success. That is a key area of focus that leaders must keep top of mind and communicate regularly to move the company forward in a productive way.

Here are a few paths to finding leadership focus:

Post your priorities: Analyze your leadership time by pinpointing the top three priorities that drive success in your business unit. Write them down, post them where you'll see them and make them part of your everyday team conversations. Keeping these touch points front-and-center will keep you—and your unit—on track amidst daily requirements. If you see your people losing focus because they have too much on their plate, remember it's your job to reorganize, regroup and re-focus individuals on those vital priorities.

Get on the same page: You know the core functions of your business better than anybody. Talk to your team about goals and direction so that everyone is starting on the same page and headed in the same direction. But don't stop there: Discuss direction and goals regularly. Repetition is crucial. Why? The human brain only recalls about 10 percent of what it hears a week later. Repeating the same information may seem like overkill but it's essential to fostering energized, dedicated teams.

Go back to basics: The best-run businesses and most successful leaders clearly articulate and underscore the organization's mission and basic value structure. Think of these set standards as the concrete blocks on which the corporate house is built; if they crumble, your house will fall down. The leaders who really accomplish great things talk about these tenets all the time. While more high-level values are important, the basics are the glue that holds everything together.

Share the results: In the retail world, selling is what we do and sales numbers are the measurement of our success. So, at Tractor Supply the first topic of the day is always sales—from yesterday's numbers to the monthly reports. We share sales numbers companywide and encourage healthy competition among stores, districts and regions. No one is confused.

In an increasingly sophisticated business environment, staying focused can be extra difficult. But in the long run creating a clear direction for your team is what it takes to achieve leadership success.

Lead with passion
NBJ September 2011

Passion is magnetic. Employees and customers gravitate to enthusiastic leaders who are genuinely excited about their job and their mission. Leaders who can show emotion become more real and human in everyone's eyes. You earn the admiration of others when you show passion—whether that's through a smile, a laugh, or even a cry. My advice is to find a variety of simple, sustainable ways to lead—and live—with passion.

Take an interest: Lead in way that will make your employees look forward to seeing you. Start by carving out a little time to show a sincere interest in your employees by asking questions about family and interests. For example, follow up on a sick relative, a child's ball game or a mother-in-law's visit. Or get more actively involved with the work your team is doing—without becoming a micro-manager. Connect meaningfully with others by being genuine and always wearing a big smile.

Engage with enthusiasm: Engage equally enthusiastically with people outside your organization: customers, business partners and prospects. Whenever you can, try visiting a customer in-person—at their place of business—and inquiring about different aspects of their company. Most people are thrilled when others show interest in *their* organizations.

Celebrate success: Be passionate about recognizing achievement. When an employee does something good, make a big deal of it. When a team achieves a milestone, celebrate in a creative way. The more unpredictable your celebration the more people will remember the event. Likewise, when you observe or hear about a customers' success, find some way to show your admiration—call, write, or send a pizza, cake or flowers. Demonstrate your passion for the achievement of others, showing a deep sense of sincere appreciation for valuable accomplishments.

Solve problems passionately: Passion works just as well in challenging times. When something goes wrong, focus on positive ways to rally others to solve the problem. Think of the dilemma as an opportunity to build an individual's confidence as well as the camaraderie of the team. Passionately committed leaders do not place blame; they seek solutions.

People take notice when you demonstrate everyday passion in your role. When you are seen as a passionate, committed leader respect will quickly flow your way.

Top 4 take-charge practices to lead your team
NBJ September 2015 (Original title: Leaders take charge)

The finest leaders I have worked with and studied from afar are clear and confident. They set unmistakable direction and paint a simple, well-defined picture for short- and long-term goals. The payoff? Every team member on a well-led team knows exactly where the train is going. Knowledgeable and prepared people accomplish more, which in turn reflects positively on the leader.

I spent half of my working life at Tractor Supply, devoting most of my time to coaching store managers and team members about how to be good leaders. It's an investment in my time that paid off in infinite ways. Here are four take-charge leadership practices that always payoff:

Empowerment: Smart leaders stay engaged with their team, but ultimately, they don't do the work or even make the decisions. Instead, attentive managers work closely with and empower the people they're leading. They push decision-making as far down the ladder as possible—to the workers who really know the products and services.

Communication: Effective leaders build a solid, trusting team atmosphere by sharing all relevant information. At Tractor Supply we prided ourselves on being a "no secrets" company, because we knew that the more people knew the sooner and more effectively, they achieved corporate goals. Withholding information only acts to undermine communication and collaboration.

Recognition: Recognizing good performance is also essential to building teamwork. A simple pat on the back can do wonders for both individual motivation and team morale. When a big success is achieved, it's time for celebration.

Time management: In addition to guiding others, leaders earn respect by taking charge of their own time. Often executives who allow assistants to schedule their calendars are left wondering why there's no time available for the highest priority tasks. Take back your time by looking at the big picture first. Months ahead, block out important priorities such as big meetings, special events, family time and vacation. Day to day, monitor your time by effectively directing meetings: 1) circulate an agenda, 2) limit time on each topic and 3) even end a few minutes early.

The most successful leaders take charge by setting well-defined direction for their teams—and themselves.

The power of leadership
NBJ November 2020

In a leadership role you probably have more power than you realize. So, use it judiciously. Heed President Teddy Roosevelt's advice from more than a century ago: "Walk softly and carry a big stick." Never use the sheer power of your leadership position if you have a softer alternative.

In fact, the most respected leaders conduct business using as little direct power as possible. Your employees already know you're charge; you have the power to set direction, conduct performance reviews, and to hire and fire.

So, there's really no excuse for micro managing or being overbearing in your relationships. This is particularly important when you are in your first leadership role because you only have one shot to set the tone. Leaders who exercise more power than is absolutely necessary often alienate people they need most—their team.

Setting direction: Your real power comes in your ability to set the right direction for your organization and then to sell your vision to your team. Corporate leadership may set your goals for you; or you may set your own. More likely it is a combination. Either way, your job is to define and build a plan that sets clear direction for the organization.

The most effective plans are easily understood, clearly measurable and regularly reportable to everyone involved. When your business plan is in good shape, has been reviewed by key people and is ready to go, only then it is time to move on to the next step—selling it.

Communicating the plan: Most people anxiously await your plan because it's part of their livelihood. Your role as a leader is to define, explain and sell the plan. Keep it simple, avoiding unnecessary technical terms. Speak intentionally and repeat yourself more than you think you need to. It usually takes time and discussion for people to grasp the plan. Deliver your talk as frequently as necessary and leave plenty of time for questions and discussion. The more thoroughly the plan is understood the better the execution.

When plans involve change, which most do, you can expect some degree of anxiety on the part of the folks impacted. The greater the degree of change the more of your time you may need to devote to communication.

Dealing with conflict: Part of your role as a leader is dealing with differences of opinion. Sometimes disparities can evolve into serious conflict, which you are also obligated to resolve. Listen carefully, discuss the issues and try not to show favoritism. Sometimes the resolution is easy and sometimes you simply have to make a decision among two or more options.

Act prudently. If you move too quickly you may create additional tension, but if you act too slowly your people may see you as weak. These are times when a good mentor can help guide you down the best path.

Staying calm: Leaders know how to keep their cool—no matter what. You don't want to be in a situation where you panicked under pressure and made a bad decision that must be rescinded later. When in doubt, take more time.

I learned this on the job. On one memorable occasion I became so emotional about a particular topic that I spouted off instead of keeping my mouth shut. I should have slowed down, reflected and not acted on emotion. My solution? Take a 30-minute walk. You may find, like me, that you return with a very different perspective. Another idea: Sleep on it. When you're upset or under pressure, do not make a major decision without at least one night's space. It can work wonders.

Remember, as a leader you have a lot of power. So, use it responsibly.

Leaders push teams to always improve, evolve
NBJ October 2011

The old adage "If it ain't broke, don't break it" just doesn't fly in today's marketplace. Our world is moving at warp-speed, and competition is tougher than ever. As our competitors work diligently to improve, we must work even harder to innovate and advance faster to stay ahead of the pack. Strong companies and good leaders know that to compete in the modern free market the best approach is really more like: "If it ain't broke, let's break it and make it better."

If we do what we've always done we stifle innovation and quickly lose ground. Progress is a direct result of continuous change and an unrelenting commitment to improvement. Jumpstart a more competitive, creative and stimulating workplace environment with these simple tips:

Curiosity: Demonstrate and encourage everyday curiosity among your team by asking questions, challenging the status quo and always seeking out ways to improve your business. People who are consistently curious will challenge current processes and products, and ultimately push forth new ideas that can build a stronger, more successful company.

Innovation: Be a champion of innovation in your organization. Create an open, inspired environment that's conducive to innovation—new ideas are the lifeblood of a growing and changing business. Support, encourage and protect those mavericks who have initial ideas that may seem a little "off the wall." Often those type of suggestions lead to new and better products and services. Forget how it was done it in the past. Look at how you can do it better in the future.

The people's ideas: In most businesses the best ideas come from those who are closest to the work. That means your team—the people who are out in the field or talking to customers daily. Our role as leaders is to encourage our people to suggest the ideas and changes that can realistically improve our product or service.

Listen to your team and push forward those little sparks of brilliance that will make your company even better.

Process improvement: Best-practice teams that focus on key issues often unlock the secrets that lead to greater efficiency in even the simplest tasks. And you don't have to micro-manage them. These smart, self-starting teams typically achieve the most when we just leave them alone to brainstorm. "We are taking notes but not taking names," I used to tell these teams. When change makes a measurable difference, be sure to celebrate it, too. The more positive change is recognized and rewarded the more constructive change you will see.

Business is always changing in a perpetual quest to improve. The secret to success is simple: The best organizations innovate smarter and change faster than the competition.

Leadership wins with trust, empowerment
NBJ October 2013 (Original title "Win with trust")

Want to win in a leadership role? Learn to trust your team, peers and business partners. When delegating responsibility, the most powerful and motivating words you can utter are "I trust you." Creating an environment of trust builds confident, self-motivated and inspired teams that don't require micro managing. Research shows that organizations and leaders that are trusted have lower employee turnover, higher revenue growth and greater profitability. So how do you get started?

Start with a two-step engagement process: professional and personal. First, talk to team members about specific job responsibilities and how each person goes about getting things done. Listen with sincere interest. Ask questions, learn and show you support them. After all, it's your responsibility to see that your people get the tools, training and encouragement to excel. Then ensure your team's interests are aligned with the company's goals.

Now that you are functionally engaged with your team, it's time to build deeper trust by engaging more personally. Pay attention to the special talents and quirks of every individual, and give honest, thorough and frequent performance feedback. Early constructive discussions on difficult issues work best. Talk periodically to each person about his or her career goals, and don't assume they're the same as what you remember from a conversation two years ago. When it comes to career growth you are the most important person in the loop and can probably provide the most effective career development coaching.

Whether engaging on a professional or personal level, your most important trust-building skill as a leader of people is communication. Keep no secrets. Be honest and upfront. Speak frequently about the issues and values that are most important. If there are black clouds on the horizon, be sure to do the talking before rumors beat you to it. Trusted leaders always communicate ahead of the grapevine.

Remember, all of your words and actions are observed, so do what you say. When you make a commitment, people expect you to follow through. If something comes up that prevents you from honoring your word explain the situation in as much detail as necessary so your team understands the circumstances. When you are open about issues people understand, but if you ignore or bury the topic people will become distrustful.

So, start with "I trust you" and then watch the faces on your team light up. Your stars will rise—and so will your wins.

Trust your team and get out of the way
NBJ—January 2014 (Originally Delegate your way to success)

The most effective business leaders amass the right people, set clear direction and then empower a team to get the job done. After more than 50 years in business, I've deduced from study and observation that the principal obstacle to solid executive growth is the inability to effectively delegate. When you think "I can do it better myself," you may have plateaued in your career. Leaders must learn to be good delegators.

Micromanaging is the No. 1 morale killer in any organization. Leaders win when people—not the boss—accomplish the work. Look at the big picture and stay out of the minutiae to find the path to true leadership. A mix of instincts and work experience will help you decide where and when to delegate.

Many years ago, I had a mentor who likened business leaders to orchestra conductors. Your role is to get all these different people to play all these different instruments (think business tasks) so that the final product is beautifully in tune. Most importantly, he pointed out: An orchestra leader seldom plays an instrument.

I credit much of my success to assigning responsibilities to a trusted team, with minimal follow up. Delegating responsibility to strong subordinates is essential to your ability to effectively manage any operation. However, delegating too much to new, inexperienced or under-qualified people can lead to serious issues. Place clear responsibilities on the backs of your key team members so you will have time and peace of mind to see "over the hill and around the corner." When you are able to look into the future you are moving into the ranks of the truly great leaders.

As you mature in your leadership role you will feel more and more comfortable saying the magic words of delegation: I trust you. Once you master the trust factor you are preparing for the next level of leadership. Build trust, delegate intelligently and then get out of the way. That's when magic things happen.

Leaders must get out of their offices
NBJ May 2017 (original title: Keep moving to keep learning)

If you want to truly lead, you can't do it sitting on the sidelines. The most effective leaders I know seem to be in perpetual motion. But they certainly are not spinning in circles. These movers and shakers spend time wisely with key people, business functions and new projects. They know that the more business operations they interact with, the more knowledge they will gain. And it's the most active, informed people who give themselves the best chance at becoming great leaders.

When I think about intelligently active leaders, there's one example that always comes to mind: a friend and manager of a large, multi-factory manufacturing company who always seems to be on the move. He starts each morning in the factory by reviewing current plant productivity with leadership teams. Then he walks the floor, talking to employees about workflow, new ideas, culture, family and just about any other topic that might impact productivity. By staying plugged in, he's become a pro at identifying small issues before they become big problems. Hands-on mentoring is his special way of coaching supervisors to be effective in their roles.

I, too, stayed active in my role at Tractor Supply. More than half of my working days were spent on the road in our stores with two or three associates. We listened, asked questions, demonstrated support and often waited on customers. We made visits to three or four stores a day and were in perpetual motion learning about people, products and processes.

We also made full-day visits to our distribution centers, where we soaked up everything, we could in a quest to provide the stores with the best possible support. On other occasions we spent several days at trade shows, studying new products and meeting current and potential suppliers.

This constant motion—and knowledge gain—yielded the information we needed to make the best possible decisions and set the clearest direction for the organization. The overarching goal was to continually improve every aspect of the business.

Over the years, I also carved out time to do some serious leadership coaching. Here are some of the things I shared and continue to advocate about always staying on the move as leader.

1. Heed this old adage: Inspect what you expect. You can't easily inspect from behind a desk. Get up from the behind the computer and roam around—check on things and make sure jobs are being performed.

2. Talk to your people and discuss standards and expectations. Heck, strike up a conversation with anyone who is available. You'll be amazed by not only what you can impart, but also what you can learn along the way.
3. Go to all departments and move out of your comfort zone. I gained so much by just walking and talking to people all over the building, from the mailroom and accounting to IT and HR. There is something to be learned everywhere.

Remember, staying plugged in is a key to leadership success. Keep moving so you can keep learning.

Activity isn't accomplishment
NBJ October 2015; (Originally "Don't confuse activity with accomplishment")

Activity—doing stuff—is not and never will be a form of accomplishment. I learned that over the years, but never so clearly as one evening when I was in charge of a 20-person, front-end retail operation. As the store was closing, I pitched in to help load paper bags at the checkouts. About five minutes into this task, the store manager put his big hand on my shoulder and discreetly pulled me aside.

He pointed to three young guys sitting on checkout #20 laughing and joking. He explained that I had been given the opportunity to lead, not just work. He challenged me to think of myself as an orchestra leader who has to get all the different personalities to play a lot of different instruments to achieve a pleasant tune. I realized right then that my job was leading, not accomplishing individual tasks. That night I became a true delegator—one of the skills that helped me most in my career.

Busy may not be constructive: Leadership is a learned art. And before we recognize its nuances, many of us fall back on trying to "busy" ourselves in effort to look productive, but these menial or misguided tasks rarely produce real results or change. If at the end of the day you can't effectively pinpoint your accomplishments as a leader over the activity you engaged in, you may want to reassess your allocation of time.

Here's a scenario about telling the difference. Let's assume you are the manager of a Tractor Supply store. At 6 p.m. on day one you look back and note that you helped unload a truck, stocked shelves in the pet food area and recorded low-inventory items in the tool section. You worked with a number of customers and actually sold a $2,500 tractor. You have certainly done a lot of work, but the activities are primarily tasks of a standard salesperson, so your management accomplishments are minimal.

On day two you take a different approach. You start by setting clear work assignments; post and discuss the day's sales goals; and verbally recognize everyone who has worked toward achieving those objectives. Next you study current profit data and take action based on those indicators. If sales in a particular category have been declining recently you study the data, review the merchandise presentation, talk with the right sales people to ascertain the reason and put in place a plan to reverse the decline. Later you set aside 30 minutes to work with your newest team members on the company's mission and values. At the end of the day, you see that you guided people in achieving goals, initiated a data-driven solution to address a sales issue and helped coach new employees. This is real management accomplishment.

At the end of every workday take stock of your accomplishments. If you do this regularly, you will quickly ascertain the difference between activity and accomplishment. And, trust me, you will want more of the latter.

Be direct in your business: it's a winning formula
NBJ August 2019

Throughout my career I have always tried to be direct in my business dealings. I learned early in life that sugarcoating issues is simply a delay tactic. Eventually you have to face reality. To be effective we all need accurate and complete information. Without it, we run the risk of making poorly informed decisions. And those tend to boomerang on you. The best way to solve problems is to address them head on with all the unvarnished facts on the table.

I was lucky to learn the value of frankness from two different leaders early in my career. While their styles were unique, they were both very direct with me. Their constructive coaching and fact-based criticism helped me become a more effective leader.

I also learned directness on the job—from my own employees. For example, on more than one occasion a young woman on my team dropped into my office and said something to this effect: "Do you realize the impact of what you said to Frank this morning?" Clearly, I didn't. But her directness gave me the opportunity to apologize and clarify something that was not received positively.

I will forever be grateful. You can best lead when you have associates who feel free to give you tough feedback. I've since tried to pass down what I absorbed over the years about the value of directness in business.

Talking to your team: There is great potential in being straight with the folks who work for you. Directness is a reflection of honesty, a quality that builds greater mutual respect. So don't beat around the bush about individual and team performance issues. Review the facts, plan your discussion and start communicating. When you help your team members perform more effectively you all win.

Being clear with business partners: Shooting straight with those you deal with outside your organization is also a winning formula. When either side holds back, an aura of distrust clouds the business dealing, which can only confuse and potentially ruin the relationship. Both sides function best with clear, timely and direct communication.

Sharing knowledge with your boss: I know that most of the best ideas in our company come directly from those closest to the work. So don't be shy about sharing. Your boss will be at his or her best when working with complete and accurate information, so it helps both you and your higher up. Good leaders want to hear from the team, so be direct in sharing your forward-looking thoughts about any important aspect of work operations.

Delivering bad news: Everyone wants to hear good news, but sometimes we have an obligation to deliver bad news. Our unit will perform best when we have all the facts and can make the best decisions possible. Plan the delivery of the tough stuff carefully and thoroughly, but don't wait. Delaying sharing unpleasant news often makes it worse in the long run. Gather the facts and your courage—and get it over with.

Discussing performance reviews: Most of us dread and often postpone difficult employee performance discussions. Again, don't procrastinate. You can bet your employee knows it is coming and will be equally happy to put it in the history books. The best tactics for reviews are to research your points; stick to the facts; avoid generalized words like always and never; and don't get emotional.

I know it always makes me feel good when people thank me for being direct. It's a sign of respect. Not everyone is anxious to hear the truth, but in the long run accurate information delivered upfront is best for all concerned. Being direct in all your communications will put you on a positive path to leadership success.

Succession plan: leaders develop the next wave of talent
NBJ Feb 2019 (original title: Leaders Develop Leaders)

Nearly all the lessons I've learned about developing leaders came the hard way. And that's why they sunk in. I started accruing much of this knowledge early on in my retail career.

In my mid-twenties, I was tasked with supervising checkout managers, as well as cash-handling sections of large discounts stores. I was full of energy, the youngest guy on the team and single. So, leadership assigned me the broadest geography, which required the most driving. (The company would seldom spring for airfare.) My stores—about a dozen at the time—were spread from Buffalo to Baltimore.

When I had a dozen solid store managers life was good. But that was not always the case. If one of my managers quit, the replacement just might be me. I soon realized that my clearest path to success was to build bench strength so if we lost a manager for any reason, we had a backup somewhere in the wings.

I refined my recruiting and interviewing skills mostly through trial and error. Then I learned to be a one-man training machine. Over time many of the folks I developed moved on to bigger roles both in our company in other organizations.

Creating a pipeline of new leadership talent: Today well-run organizations of all sizes have learned the same thing I did: Developing fresh leaders is just as valuable as managing existing leaders. Companies now invest heavily in all aspects of leadership development, because they know that in the long run talent could be the most critical competitive advantage.

Regular assessments are a key tool for fostering leadership talent at every level. It's essential for senior executives, including the CEO, to ask tough questions to build a resilient team.

- Who are the "stars" and how are we preparing them for the future?
- Who are the "backbone" managers and are we providing them with solid support?
- Are we counseling our "problem" managers adequately?
- Do we have enough talent in the pipeline and is it the right talent?

Forward-thinking businesses know that resources spent on skill development will pay off in two important ways: stronger leaders and deeper loyalty to the organization. In fact, tailoring programs for your most promising individuals can deliver huge dividends.

Leadership training comes in many forms and usually works best as a complementary mix of programming. This could include individual skill classes (public speaking, organization, managing people), in-house group classes, new "challenge" projects and networking opportunities.

Our spin on leadership training: Tractor U: Building on this idea, our team started Tractor Supply University, fondly known as Tractor U. The leadership training content, much of it delivered by senior executives, continues to evolve. But the singular intention remains the same: a dedication to building a first-class leadership team. Tractor U teaching has led directly to high loyalty and very low turnover.

When you think about your own progression as a leader, ask yourself this: Who have I groomed to take my place? Your prospects for promotion grow when you make life easy by introducing your boss to your trained successor.

Luckily, I learned the value of talent early on. I worked relentlessly to select the best people for key corporate roles. I spent a huge portion of my time teaching in classrooms and coaching in stores far and wide. Why? Because I knew that leadership development was the very best investment of my time.

Leaders deliver bad news
NBJ April 2019

Nobody likes delivering bad news. But there are times when leaders must do the hard work. Sometimes the tough topic is employee performance or a structural change in the organization. It could be an operational catastrophe or any raft of other issues that come along with managing people in the workplace.

Like all companies, Tractor Supply had its share of bad news to deliver. For example, when I joined the organization, I knew the company soon would be relocating from Chicago to one of four cities.

As the new vice president of personnel, it was my job to manage much of this transition process, including shutting down a rumor mill gone wild. In this case, honest communication paid off.

THE CULTURE WARRIOR

First, we confirmed with staff the relocation site: Nashville. Then we announced dates for the next steps. Some personnel were invited to move. Others could take advantage of severance packages and employment-assistance programs. With the clear communication, there was nothing left to talk about. We all got back to work—and almost every employee stayed during the final months in Chicago.

Twenty years later we had outgrown our Indianapolis distribution center. Not surprisingly, productivity had declined. But the grapevine spun a story before we made our final construction commitment. Without a known location, I had to explain to both shifts the necessity for a larger facility, even though we didn't know where that would be! With the quick and honest communication, productivity stabilized and only a couple employees left during the time of uncertainty.

I learned a lot from these experiences—and many more that followed. Here are some tips that might help leaders navigate the choppy waters of change:

1. **Don't panic:** Sit back and think through the issues. Develop a methodical and logical approach to delivering the bad news. Think about the result you expect to achieve. Then work backward through the actions you must take to achieve that result. Plan carefully and when possible, work with trusted associates. Solid preparation is the best way to keep things from falling off the rails.
2. **Don't procrastinate:** Bad news usually gets worse, and in some cases much worse, if you "wait it out." You can't put it aside and hope it might go away. To show true leadership in the face of adversity, you must take charge. Address the issue maturely, directly and with a sense of urgency.
3. **Don't speculate:** Often the bad news leaders have to deliver relates to poor employee performance. Start by reviewing the facts. Verify that you have all the pertinent, accurate information in hand. Plan your conversation carefully and set a time to talk. Stick to the facts, stay positive and don't

get emotional. But don't forget to listen carefully, because there may be more to the story than you realized. Outline the next steps and work toward a conclusion that you can both agree on.

As leaders it's often our responsibility to deliver unpleasant messages. But keep an open mind. Once people hear the truth, they often bond to help the whole organization get through the challenges ahead. So, when it's your turn to deliver bad news, plan your communication carefully, and deliver it as honestly and quickly as you can. And for big announcements always try to beat the grapevine. Good luck!

Time not on your side—take control
NBJ July 2010

Time is a perishable commodity for all of us. Good planning on your part and a sincere respect for the time of those around you will help you get the most out of the limited time available. Following are a few key thoughts:

Plan ahead: Maintain a forward-looking list of important tasks, events and goals and assign each to specific future weeks and months. Review your plan regularly making adjustments as needed and building the current and upcoming week's plan by day.
Plan your day: At the end of each work day take a few minutes to review your calendar for the next few days to make sure all is scheduled, planned and prepared. You will sleep better and get a faster start the next day when you have a solid plan ready to go.
Appointments: Be on time and be prepared. Confirm the agenda and time allocation at the beginning of the appointment and then you will be more productive and end on schedule. If your appointment is significantly late, take the initiative to reschedule rather than have the rest of your day in turmoil.

Drop ins: When you drop in to see someone or someone drops by to see you take the initiative to set the framework right away. Discuss the topic and time needed, and proceed if you both agree. If not, schedule a specific future time and place.

Telephone conversations: When you make the call start with "Hello Joe, I need to discuss the 'X project' and need about ten minutes of your time." You can then jointly decide whether to talk now or schedule a later call. Follow the same process when you receive an unexpected call.

Conference calls and meetings: When you are in charge circulate an agenda with specific times for each topic at least one day in advance. Ask for comments and adjust the agenda based on the feedback. You are now armed with a timed agenda which is the tool that allows you to keep things moving on schedule. If you are a participant, you also can ask for an agenda in advance.

E-mails: Less is good. Short is essential. "cc" is most often just wasting someone's time. Be prudent. You don't win popularity contests sending emails. If the topic is important don't waste time on email—go down the hall or get on the phone to resolve the issue.

The better you manage your time the more productive you will be. The better you help to manage other people's time the more respect you will earn. Take charge of your time—it is one thing you really can manage.

How to run a big meeting (or even a small one)

NBJ July 2015 (Orig. Are you running a big meeting? Or even a small one?)

If you are in a leadership role the chances are that you will be called on from time to time to oversee and run big sales and business meetings of one kind or another. At this point you have an opportunity to shine or fall on your face. The first option is generally preferred. Here are some of my thoughts about meeting organization that might help you shine.

Plan: The first step is to plan your meeting carefully. Draft the agenda, share it with key constituents and ask for comments. Finalize your agenda including time allocations for each topic and speaker. Share the agenda again so that when the time comes there are no surprises.

Take charge: When the meeting is in process it is up to you as the leader to keep things running on time which may include politely pushing the group to move on to the next topic. You will be remembered for your organization, content of the subjects and for your punctuality. The group will love you if your meeting ends a little early and feel the opposite if you let things drag on way past your scheduled quitting time.

Practice: Big meetings involving multiple speakers usually need some practice which can make all the difference in the world. If you have acknowledged experienced speakers make sure the time limit is understood in advance. If you are working with less experienced folks practice and sometimes lots of it can really help. The opening and closing usually comments need the most rehearsal. If you or your speakers are using humor, make sure the jokes are really funny— nothing can erode speaker confidence faster than a joke gone badly.

Nervous speaker: Reassure your speaker that no one in the audience can tell that she is nervous. Reassure her that she is the authority on the subject—that way she was chosen. Plus, you have herd her rehearse several times and she is a "star."

Support materials: Be sure videos, PowerPoints, etc. are fully functional and tested several times prior to the meeting. Keep visual aids simple and understandable. PowerPoints should be kept to a limited number of pages and no more than a half dozen bullet points on a page. If handouts are part of the meeting they should be distributed at the end. Remember that your speaker is the "star attraction' not the visuals and the handouts.

Q & A portion: If you plan on a question-and-answer session let the audience know ahead of time so they prepare during the talk. Asking "what questions do you have" generally garners quicker participation than "do you have questions." Always repeat the question for the audience.

Preparation: If it is a big meeting get there early. Check all the technical support—microphones, video, etc. Make sure there is water for the speaker. Get comfortable with the surroundings.

Leaders establish their credentials by running effective meetings. Next time you get the chance show them how well you can do!

Overcome outsized ego and the need to do it all
NBJ Feb 2015 (Original title "Overcome leadership obstacles")

Two of the biggest obstacles to good leadership practices are an outsized ego and a reluctance to delegate.

Stay humble, stay successful: We are not born with big egos but they can develop over time if we are not careful and well disciplined. Inflated egos often expand slowly with a big success or two, and confidence grows a little faster than it should. With continued success, ego can bloat even further and truly distort self-image. At this point, you are most likely going to alienate some of your key associates and maybe even lose a few friends.

At the same time, people often tell egoists what they think they want to hear, and sooner or later show boaters become isolated from reality. I recall one sad case where a CEO stopped eating in lunchroom in favor of a private dining room; then stopped driving his car in favor of a company limo; and then hired a bodyguard. He became so out of touch that his entire company began to stumble as a result. His days were numbered.

The antidote to an inflated ego? Never let your success go to your head. We are all human. We all achieve in exceptional ways. Keep your victories to yourself or graciously accept praise from others who acknowledge your success. My advice is simple: Stay humble, stay connected and stay employed.

Delegate your way to success: The fastest way to turn off your people is to become a micromanager. Like the ego, this kind behavior, such as monitoring every employee action and criticizing work, can creep up slowly. Don't let it. Micro-managing sends a clear message of distrust, and in that environment, there is typically little or no teamwork, zero creativity and high turnover. That is a guaranteed trajectory to failure.

The antidote to micromanagement? Build trust by delegating. Start by surrounding yourself with the right people. Then set clear direction, provide only essential support and keep your message consistent: "I trust you." Follow this approach and you will earn the respect of your team, and results will follow.

Empowered people will put forth the ideas to help business prosper, often becoming the leaders of the future. And you can set that in motion. When leaders delegate effectively, they have time to do what leaders are supposed to do—look over the hill and around the corner—not over shoulders.

Remember, a big ego will isolate and micromanaging will alienate. Stay humble, delegate effectively and you will find the right kind of success.

In trouble? Be proactive
NBJ June 2018

When we are in trouble at work our natural tendency is to run for cover—stick our head in the sand—and hope it will all go away. While this approach might work to temporarily assuage the situation, the issue will likely linger.

Many years ago, a mentor of mine taught me a great lesson: It's when you are in trouble that you need to communicate the most. He coached that the best long-term resolutions are achieved by having a proactive, in-depth conversation—not running away from the issue.

Conflict with the boss: Early in my career a friend passed along a rumor he heard that my boss was getting ready to fire me. I instinctively charged into my boss's office and confronted him—not pleasant for either of us. He was frustrated with me and had begun to seek a replacement. After several long talks over the next few days, we resolved the issues and reconstructed the relationship in a positive way.

This kind of thing happens all the time in the workplace. Let's say you really screwed something up and the boss chewed you out, which was upsetting but certainly well deserved. You go home that evening, complain to your spouse, toss and turn all night, and wake up still upset. What next?

My advice is to do a clear-headed analysis of the facts and then put it all down in writing. Study what happened and make an appointment to see the boss. If your boss is not in town and most of the conflict occurred via email culminating in one very harsh phone call at the end of the day—wait until you are calm to analyze and plan. Then book a face-to-face with the boss. If you can't see the boss directly shoot for a FaceTime session. And if it has to be a phone call schedule enough time to talk it out properly.

Review the facts with your boss, outline a realistic plan to correct the current situation, explain your future actions to prevent a reoccurrence and offer an apology. In most cases this should be sufficient for resolution.

Issues with peers: On another early-career occasion, I lost my cool with a peer over a relatively insignificant issue. It was during a period of significant company transition—everyone was uptight and working against tough deadlines. I was off base and knew it.

Two hours later, I swallowed my pride, walked into his office and apologized for my actions. Over time we rebuilt our relationship. Had I not been proactive, we may have been walking on eggshells for months to come.

Handling peer conflicts is really no different than dealing with a boss. Take time to calm down and organize your thoughts. Then schedule a time for a genuine conversation. An apology, hopefully on both sides, plus a firm handshake will typically put the issue in the history bin.

It is essential to resolve significant workplace issues as quickly as you can. Simmering tensions may go away in the short term, but they tend to boil up over time. Be proactive in seeking resolution for all conflict.

Tips for leading in uncertain times
NBJ April 2020

This is one of the most unusual times of our lives. And now is when leaders should step up like never before. Our people, peers and even superiors need to see us as calm, mature and engaged—even in the face of tragedy. True leaders will not panic, but rather move forward as balanced business managers and executives.

We all know that the quality and cohesiveness of our team is critical to long-term success. Whether your team is still with you or on furlough, it is essential to stay plugged in to provide as much grounding and consistency as possible. In all likelihood your people are feeling extraordinarily insecure right now and need to see you as rock solid.

Hopefully you will all be back working together in a normal environment in the not-too-distant future. But during this most trying period, your team needs your guidance and demonstrable ways to reflect on your actions with pride and respect.

You can never over-communicate in crisis: Now is the time to communicate like never before. Listen to everyone's concerns and only react when you are confident in your words and actions. In tough times sincere listening may be the very best thing you can do. Remain calm, open and honest. Don't keep secrets. Communicate news efficiently in an evenhanded manner—don't act excited or scared. And to reduce the rumor mill, try your best to ensure that news gets to everyone about the same time.

Misinformation can create chaos. Don't share anything but the undisputed data. If some information floating around sounds fishy, use your time to uncover the facts and then share with your team. If you think it is advantageous to offer your trusted opinion, make doubly sure that everyone understands that it is indeed *your* view. Build greater credibility by communicating honestly, fairly and, whenever possible, quickly.

If you were required to furlough some or most of your staff, find ways to stay in touch. They still need to hear from you. E-mail is easiest: Send regular messages of fact and hope. Let your people know you are concerned about them and their families. Try mailing a weekly status sheet to their homes. Sign each one and, if you can, add a few words of your own. If you have time an occasional phone call can be very powerful for building loyalty and cementing the long-term bond.

Stay current and connected: Stay plugged in to current events surrounding coronavirus. The goal is not to be an authority on the pandemic, but rather to have a sharp, high-level understanding of its impact on people and business. At this point facts matter most; gossip will only fuel anxiety. Listen carefully to be sure people are not getting wound up over misguided notions or disparate details.

Stay on top of daily developments in your organization—and your industry. Clear, consistent and factual communication of this information will build confidence in the future and may allay common fears.

Your demeanor during uncertain times means everything in the eyes of your people and those in your organization. If you appear stressed or panicked, people around you will lose confidence and look elsewhere for leadership. On the other hand, if you are seen as stable, mature and calm in spite of all that is happening you will earn confidence and respect. Now is the time when quality leadership shines through and can be a bright spot for all.

Plan for the future: Share everything you can about both current and future events, particularly those that can build confidence in a return to normal. But be sure to paint a realistic, not overly optimistic, picture of what's to come.

It is never too early to begin planning a return to normality. Start on it now. Engage your people: Decide what items of business need to get done first and who will do them. Then draft assignments and schedules for the first few weeks back to work. Let your people see that there is a future and you are all planning for it.

Your team is looking to you for purpose. These are the times when true leadership rises to the surface. Be calm. Be clear. Be compassionate. Be the ultimate communicator.

I have been through several wars, 9/11 and a few massive market crashes. And I can say with confidence that this pandemic has been the most rapid destabilizer of all. Yet, in my opinion, we will emerge from this setback, probably earlier than the pessimists say, and stronger than ever.

6. ETHICS

Open letter to business leaders
June 2009

Hello business leader,

The most admired business leaders continually demonstrate the highest level of ethical behavior in both words and actions. Leaders talk about ethical performance; leaders speak out when things seem to be headed the wrong way and leaders encourage the highest standards of ethical behavior from everyone on the team.

We all face ethical dilemmas in life—I have certainly faced my fair share. Our decisions should always be within the law and follow the basic rules set forth by business and our organizations. But it is not just about following the rules and obeying the law—it is about doing what is really right. Even when you think no one is watching. You must feel comfortable with each of your decisions.

Integrity is defined as adherence to moral and ethical principles, soundness of moral character, and honesty. Whether you are leading a team, or raising a family, your personal integrity ultimately defines who you are, and what you stand for.

The recent financial events impact virtually all of us in both our professional and personal lives. Much of the meltdown can be attributed to a lack of common sense coupled with ethical lapses. Certainly, no one wanted to wind up in the mess we find ourselves in today. Let's hope we are now on the road to recovery.

The purpose of this letter is to remind us all about the importance of personal integrity in all we do no matter the outside influences. It is also to remind you that our capitalist economic system is the world's greatest wealth generator and has a historic and natural process of boom-and-bust cycles. We will emerge from this cycle, like all others, stronger than ever.

No shortcuts to higher ground
NBJ September 2011

Theft, bribery, financial manipulation, infidelity: Media stories portray a huge lapse in professional ethics, common sense and responsibility. But whether the times are really changing or we're just over-exposed to media, the publicity of moral mishaps is undoubtedly deterring the business community from committing misdeeds. The ethical bar has been raised.

So, it's back to Ethics 101: True leaders don't take shortcuts to moral high ground. They act personally and professionally with the highest degree of integrity because they know that is the only path to long-term success. They do not bend in the face of temptation. They set direction—the moral compass—and do everything possible to ensure the success of the entire organization.

Communicate clearly. Repeat: A big part of maintaining high ethical standards starts with thorough and regular communication. Avoid costly and stressful misunderstandings by being clear about expectations. Frequently talk about the importance of taking honest and ethical actions. Experts say that we are lucky to recall 10 percent of what we hear, so it's a leader's responsibility to be repetitive about topics that are critically important to the reputation of an organization and its people.

Set the example: What if those around you aren't following the moral compass? That's the ideal opportunity to step up and be a true leader by both clearly setting the right example and then challenging those who chose not to walk the high road. Ethical leadership is a wining practice, and you can lead the way. Those of us in leadership roles have a solemn obligation to set the moral tone for our people. In the end, leaders who take the high road earn the most respect and, in the long term, are the most successful.

Take action when necessary: Inevitably at some point as a leader you may work for a higher-up who does not always exemplify the right behavior. While this can seem like a tough situation, I can tell you with confidence, as a former CEO, that senior leaders in almost every organization *want* to follow the right path. Sometimes they just need a little nudge in the right direction. Your challenge is to approach your boss in a constructive way or, depending on the circumstances, take the matter through the right corporate channels for resolution. Demonstrating your own sense of moral direction can guide others down the same path.

Business leaders must promote integrity, ethics
2009

The topic of ethics belongs at the top of our national agenda. Now is the time for our political, spiritual and business leaders to raise the national bar on integrity. The ethical lapses that seem so prevalent today always come back to haunt the initiators. The rewards, both personal and professional, for moral and ethical business leadership are great and the consequences of falling short are enormous. Straighten up, America!

Pfizer has agreed to pay $2.3 billion dollars for illegally marketing a painkiller.

The story goes like this. Pharmaceutical companies are authorized by the Food and Drug Administration to sell their medicines for specific uses. In this case, Pfizer somehow marketed this product for unapproved uses. It would be understandable (not acceptable) if one or two inexperienced sales people got carried away and marketed the product for the wrong uses. But when the settlement is in the **billions** of dollars, it becomes obvious that the ethical breakdowns were very broad-based.

ow can an ethical breakdown be so great that it can cost $2.3 billion? It is apparent that the leadership is either disconnected from the business or just plain think they are above the law. Stakeholders should not tolerate that brand of leadership. We should all speak-out in opposition to any and every ethical lapse from any American business.

The popular response to ethical business lapses is a call for more regulation. After Enron, World.Com, Tyco and the others, the government gave us the Sarbanes-Oxley Act. Sarbanes-Oxley has cost US businesses (and, in turn, consumers) billions in bureaucratic controls, made us that much less competitive, driven most IPOs offshore and has done little or nothing to stop fraud and dishonesty. Morality, honesty, integrity and ethics are human values that are almost impossible to regulate.

Our political, spiritual and business leaders should encourage and celebrate ethics and integrity at every opportunity. Doing the right thing all the time, regardless of the consequences, should be the standard for American business. We, as citizens and stockholders, should hold our leaders accountable and never tolerate a shortfall of integrity.

Leaders from every walk of life should use their "bully pulpit" to repetitively espouse the importance of "taking the high road", in life as well as in business. Leaders have an obligation to set direction, and nothing is more important than setting high ethical standards. Repetitive discussion of the importance of integrity is the process for instilling the right values as part of our way of life.

But honestly, it goes beyond talking about high ethical standards. We must also demonstrate those standards in our actions. Remember, actions speak louder than words.

Leaders—consider yourselves challenged!

Values still matter in business: here's why
October 2018 (original title: Why values still matter in business)

Somewhere along our career paths, we all run in to an ethical roadblock. Mine came very early on in my retail career, before I was at Tractor Supply. I found myself facing some very serious moral dilemmas related to my direct report's integrity, as well as the values of his boss.

I saw no apparent logical path to follow. So went I to see the person I most trusted at the time: my dad. He had lots of business experience and wisdom earned in the banking business. We talked over the issues several times. Eventually I found a way to share my observations and suspicions with the right people in the organization. I stuck to my values and in the end the "bad guys" were fired. I never forgot that experience. While it was a tough lesson, it taught me how to walk the high road.

Later at Tractor Supply I observed the complete opposite in Tom Hennesy, my leader, partner and mentor. He constantly reminded us about the importance of integrity in both personal and business dealings. At first, I found the repetition overkill. But soon I learned why he did it. Focusing on the most important parts of professionalism worked. Tractor Supply demanded ethics and people acknowledged the gospel.

When I became president of Tractor Supply, the speeches I delivered always contained something about ethical behavior. As time went on, I included more about the values of our organization, including respecting others and yourself, working as a team, embracing change, taking the initiative and being accountable. We knew our values message was working when we began to hear those same words repeated elsewhere in the organization. Ethics became a key and growing part of our culture.

Embracing ethics in every area of business: My talks about our company's mission and values began to sound like a broken record to my ears, but it was received strongly by people throughout the organization. The more I talked the more I realized the impact of my words and decided to never slow down. Before a speech at one sales meeting a senior store manager asked if I was going to speak about our mission and values like I always did. I thought for a few seconds and responded, "Damn right I am."

Every fall several hundred Tractor Supply vendors assemble for a two-day conference to learn about the current year's business and projected plans for the upcoming year. We also spoke to that group about our values. To my initial surprise, our vendors were as engaged on the topic as our people! Later we learned that many of those CEOs followed in Tractor Supply's footsteps, spending greater amounts of time and effort speaking about values in their own companies.

There's no doubt that these discussions matter. Employees are more secure when they understand their organization's values. When values are clear and consistent, teams can work more comfortably with each other. Employees often stay at companies longer when they know that ethical leaders guide the business. Honestly, it took me a while to really understand that strong culture is built on basic values that everyone understands and believes in.

Today I often run into Tractor Supply employees and other business associates who harken back to talks we had about the importance of strong values. Integrity has staying power. If you want to be a memorable leader, never underestimate your impact when it comes to instilling the right values in your team.

Boards, stakeholders play key watchdog role
NBJ June, 2010

Are you frustrated about the ethical lapses in some of our corporations? Are you upset about Toyota's slow response to safety issues? Are you troubled by bankers taking bailouts and then lining their wallets with fat bonuses? Do you encounter ethical shortfalls in businesses you deal with? Don't just sit back—take action.

We are all stakeholders. Whether we are primarily employees, investors, business partners or members of the community, we all have some level of interest in business. In fact, you are likely already an investor in hundreds of companies through your 401(k)-retirement plan, mutual funds and other investments.

It holds true, then, that we should expect businesses to operate under the highest standards—and most of the time the business community meets that level of professionalism.

The board's role: To meet the standards stakeholders, expect, a board of directors is the ultimate control mechanism for public—and most private—companies. Owners (stockholders) elect a board of directors to be responsible for oversight of the entire organization. This group selects the leadership team, approves business plans and oversees accurate accounting of all business activities.

In this role, the board is also accountable for both the operational and ethical performance of the organization. It regularly reviews basic operations, the CEO's performance and the business culture as a whole. Every stakeholder should expect an honest effort by the board to do everything reasonable to ensure the success of the organization in achieving defined business goals.

The right path: Most of the time oversight by committee works. As a former CEO, I can tell you with a high degree of confidence that senior leaders in most organizations want to follow the right path. Quality boards of directors and first-rate leaders strive to embrace the highest level of ethical behavior. They do not bend in the face of temptation to take shortcuts. They set direction—the moral compass—and do everything possible to ensure the success of the entire organization. True leaders act personally and professionally with the highest degree of integrity because they know that is the only path to long-term success.

However there are times when leaders do not conduct business in an ethical manner, and in these situations, stakeholders cannot afford to sit on the sidelines. We all have an obligation to speak up and hold businesses accountable on behalf of all stakeholders.

Collective noise: No amount of government regulation will make a major difference in corporate oversight. The voice of the people will. In 2002, Congress passed the Sarbanes-Oxley Act to fix the ills brought on by Enron and other misguided corporate giants. Unfortunately, the ethical impact of the act on business has proven virtually non-existent. But businesses now spend billions on new bureaucratic processes that make American industry a little less competitive in the world market.

Don't count on government. Use your own voice to make a difference. Boards of directors are much like politicians in that they pay attention to the collective noise, so don't be shy about speaking up when you are concerned or see wrong-doing. You can write to an individual director or to the entire board; you can comment through a web site; or, if you own stock, you can attend the stockholders meeting.

Even if you are not a stockholder you can let your voice be heard. Search the internet using "board of directors with the company name" and you will easily find a path to comment directly to the board. This also works for foreign companies so don't be shy about speaking out.

All leaders need commentary from every possible source in order to make intelligent decisions and lead organizations in the best direction. Good directors will *want* to hear from you. It is very simple. We all win when we follow basic rules of integrity and accountability.

The importance of holding CEOs and boards accountable for performance
August 2007—TN Business Magazine January 2007

We have all read the stories about greedy CEOs earning huge incomes while other constituents suffer, about signing bonuses without performance clauses, about golden parachutes for the incompetent, etc. We read about outsized egos, free private aircraft travel, club memberships, greed, greed and more greed. It all makes us sick!

I was the Chairman and CEO of a public company for a dozen years and have a point of view about executive compensation. Pay me for results. If I produce good results for my stockholders pay me well. If company performance is fantastic pay me still more. But if performance is poor, I should suffer just like my employees and stockholders.

Several years ago, our profits fell below the previous year and my bonus was zero; I made sure everyone in our company knew that. One year the Board granted me a raise in excess of what I thought I deserved so I returned two thirds of it.

CEOs have much more impact on company results than anyone else. CEOs set the direction by making the final decisions on high level strategy. CEOs make final decisions on the choice of senior executives. CEOs set the moral compass and are the chief architects of the culture. CEOs are responsible and should be held accountable.

We all expect pay for performance, but how do we define and measure CEO performance? It varies by industry; generally, the criteria are revenue growth, profit growth, use of assets and stock performance. Performance measures vary with the longest-term measures for industries where lasting capital investment has the greatest impact. Stockholders elect Boards of Directors who are responsible for setting CEO performance measures.

When financial measures are positive the stock price generally follows and pay for performance is a fairly simple calculation. Include a degree of humility and frugality and the CEO will do well without being called "greedy." But when financial measures and the stock price move in opposite directions the Board must apply common sense logic. CEOs should not be rewarded for a rising stock price when the business is not doing well. But should CEOs be penalized for a weak stock price with solid financial results? Again, the Board must exercise its clear responsibility to do what is in the best long-term interest of the stockholders.

We can pontificate all day long about executive compensation abuse but recognize that stockholders elect Directors to the Board. And it is the Board that has absolute authority over CEO compensation.

If you are an unhappy stockholder, take action. If you think the CEO is overpaid for the performance of the company—call, write, email, blog, etc. Challenge the Board on the selection and compensation of the CEO. Marquee CEOs has high failure rates. In general, seasoned executives who have time with the organization have the highest success rate. Read the proxy issued before the annual stockholders meeting. New SEC rules now require full and clear disclosure of executive compensation. Most boards will sit up and take notice when stockholders speak up.

We must hold our Boards accountable whenever they decide to grant outrageous wealth to executives particularly in cases of weak or nonperformance. Board accountability is the path to reigning in excessive executive compensation.

THE CULTURE WARRIOR

Ethics under pressure
NBJ November 2012

Pressures to excel in business come from everywhere. It's tempting for business leaders to take unethical, and sometimes illegal, shortcuts to success. Heading down this risky path inevitably leads to disaster. Those who cheat the system and forget to follow the moral compass *all* get caught—and usually sooner rather than later.

First-rate leaders do not bend in the face of temptation to take shortcuts. They consistently embrace the highest level of ethical behavior. In my nearly five decades in business, including more than a decade as the CEO of a public company, it has never been clearer that ethical leadership is the only path to long-term success.

When business leaders fail to live up to high ethical standards, the media is always there to hold us accountable. While often creating a barrage of negative news stories, this kind of oversight is essential for making us even more diligent about walking the high road. Publicity has a way of inspiring leaders to strive for improvements that will keep their own businesses off the front page.

Why do they do it? Pressures to take shortcuts are often self-initiated in a quest to show results or by an ambition to get ahead. A little shortcut such as bending a rule, exaggerating a truth or making a minor adjustment seems so harmless the first time. But over a longer period, the little rule-benders grow, and before you know it you are trapped in your own web of deceit. And most important to remember: It never works. Everyone gets caught—by accountants, auditors, security people, and, most likely, by a co-worker with a greater sense of integrity.

Sometimes leaders become overconfident to the point that the ego takes over and they begin to believe that they are omniscient. They begin to see in their own results a sense of infallibility and then make decisions on that basis. Over time they become more and more isolated because they don't listen. Separated from reality, these leaders crash and burn fantastically when they are forced to face reality—a reality that usually results in personal crisis.

The right path: Business leaders have an obligation to their constituents—customers, employees, suppliers, stockholders—to operate in a way that is right and just for all. If behavior is unethical, business relationships deteriorate and ultimately success will sour.

It is incumbent on business leaders to act in an ethical way and continually talk about the importance of ethics in the business world. Good leaders give direction, set the moral compass, and do everything possible to ensure the success of the leadership team and the entire organization. The best leaders act personally and professionally with the highest degree of integrity because they know that it is the right path—and the only path—to continued success.

'Good guys' built U.S. powerhouse
September 2009

The free market economic system has built the wealthiest country in the world. We have literally millions of business leaders—the "good guys"—who work diligently and ethically every day with customers, employees and business partners to deliver quality goods and services.

These good guys working in our capitalist system are the unsung heroes responsible for our phenomenal long-term economic success.

The United States is arguably the most ethical country on the planet; however, we are not immune to the destruction that can be brought about by a handful of "bad guys."

The nation was recently victimized by a small group of high-profile business leaders who have done some really bad things. Several years from now, we will find that the bad guys who actually committed these crimes will go to jail, and many will serve lengthy sentences.

Let us not condemn a great system based on the conduct of a few bad individuals. There are millions of business leaders in America; only a tiny fraction ever walks down the path of dishonesty and illegality.

In the long run, the "good guys" build our economy and the "bad guys" get caught and are forced to pay the consequences.

With a handful of exceptions, our good business leaders focus on building their businesses ethically and honestly.

They practice and demonstrate the right path to success by:

- Taking a long-term view of their businesses.
- Practicing "servant leadership," always placing others' needs above their own.
- Following the Golden Rule and treating other people the same way they themselves would want to be treated.
- Recognizing that teamwork and strong business partnerships are essential.
- Observing the highest levels of ethical and moral conduct.

Our system thrives on leaders who push the envelope through innovation and creativity to build businesses within ethical and legal boundaries. Our business leaders make decisions all the time, hoping that the good decisions outnumber the bad ones. We would all lose if we try to restrict the risk-taking and entrepreneurial spirit that has built our fabulously successful economic system.

Free-market capitalism creates wealth and is the system that must be nurtured, preserved and encouraged. The overwhelming majority of our business leaders are hard-working, honest, ethical human beings trying to do the best job they can.

It is OK to criticize the "bad guys" because, quite frankly, they deserve it. More importantly, we must celebrate the successes of the "good guys," for they are the ones who have built this great country of ours and who will ensure America's place as the most successful economic machine in the history of the world.

Lose your ethics, lose your business
CITY PAPER MARCH 2008

The recent tainted meat scandal in California further demonstrates why uncompromising ethics in business is the only path to long-term business success. In all, 143 million pounds of meat were recalled because of a lapse of ethics.

Who wins in this mess? Absolutely no one.

Was it avoidable? Certainly.

Since so many of the senior executives of Enron, WorldCom, Adelphia, Tyco, etc., were exposed and subsequently jailed, you would think that every business person in America would have learned the importance of maintaining a high level of integrity in business practices.

It is a real shame that some still have not seen the light and grasped the obvious.

High standards, honesty, and ethical leadership all pay off in the long run and the opposite is simply a path to ultimate failure. Wake up, business leaders!

In February, Westland/Hallmark Meat of Chino California issued a recall for 143 million pounds of beef—six times larger than any previous recall. The company slaughtered cattle that could not walk and failed to notify an inspector, which is a clear violation.

Cattle that cannot walk have a higher risk of mad cow disease and bacterial contamination. What were they thinking?

Where was the leadership?

Federal inspectors did not identify the problem nor did the company report the problem from its own control processes.

A video provided by the Humane Society showed employees attempting to get sick cattle to stand up using forklifts, electric cattle prods and high-pressure water hoses.

And now speculation suggests that the plant will close. Owners will lose their investment; executives will lose their salaries and perks and the workers will all be unemployed.

The only good news in the story, if there is any good news, is that there have been no reports of illness or meat contamination.

Employees clearly violated the rules, so you have to ask a few questions:

Were the rules posted, communicated and discussed?

Was there a clear path to discuss and report dilemmas and violations?

Did the employees believe that the company strived to operate with a high degree of integrity in all aspects of its operations?

The obvious conclusion is that the answers to some or all of these questions is 'no.'

The ethical and moral direction in any organization must be set by the CEO and the senior executive leadership.

When that direction is set according to high standards and then communicated effectively and repetitively, the organization invariably lives by those standards.

We follow our leaders; when they set the right direction, we follow; when they set the wrong direction, or more commonly no direction, we wander into "no man's land."

Leadership in business is everything. We follow with pride and confidence when our leaders set a clear path that embraces high ethical standards. Workers at every level deserve the right to work for leaders who demonstrate business and personal integrity. CP

When businesses behave badly
NBJ 9/23/16 (Originally: Business Integrity: Another Massive Breakdown)

One of the nation's largest banks is dealing with a massive scandal affecting tens of thousands of customers. Wells Fargo, which historically has maintained a stellar reputation, is caught in a mess of monumental proportions.

So, what happened? Wells Fargo opened nearly two million credit card and deposit accounts that customers never knew about. The bank transferred funds without customers' knowledge. They also issued debit cards with pin numbers unknown to customers. Some staffers even created phony email addresses as part of the scam.

The company, which has fired 5,300 employees and started to clamp down on the bad practices, will pay a $185 million fine. But the damage is done. It will take years, if not decades, to rebuild the reputation and earn back the trust of customers. And there is no way to estimate the harm done to the morale of more than 260,000 bank employees.

Apparently, the con was created to achieve sales targets that would later yield incentive bonuses. Offering financial incentives to attain revenue goals is a common practice in many if not most businesses. But at Wells Fargo it blew up.

What leaders can learn from companies behaving badly: As a former executive of Tractor Supply, I know that sales and profit incentives are core to culture and essential to operations. In fact, our most common corporate conversations are about sales results. Selling is what we do and measuring sales is our most visible report card. But cheating with sales results is a conversation we never want to have.

To work properly, sales incentives should function in three healthy ways:

1. **Customers first:** The customer has to come first in any sales organization that intends to develop long-term customer relationships, which certainly include banking and retailing.
2. **Driven by data:** Sales incentives are most effective when metrics are clear, well known and ethically tied the mutual benefit of the customer and the company.
3. **Ethics above all:** If anything transpires that deceives or cheats the customer, the long-term relationship is destined to collapse. Wells Fargo's business crisis is obviously the result a large-scale cultural breakdown.

In all organizations, cultural standards must start at the top. It's the board's responsibility to ensure that the company and employees are held to the highest standards of ethical behavior. It's also the board's responsibility to hold the CEO and senior leadership accountable for company-wide communication about culture. Messages should occur with such intensity and frequency that no employee should be in doubt when it comes to standards of ethical behavior and sales performance.

Whether leadership is complicit or simply in the dark is not terribly important. The issue is that in Wells Fargo's case there was a massive cultural breakdown that rests at the doorstep of corporate leaders. There is no more important role of senior leadership than to create a top-quality culture.

Wherever you are in your leadership career—a new frontline supervisor or experienced CEO—your people need to hear from you regularly about importance of values in your organization. Teams need to know the rules and expectations. Employees must be clear about where the organization stands on important issues. And everyone needs to see you modeling the behavior that is expected.

The lessons here are very clear: A strong ethical culture is an essential building block of success. Incentives must be structured in an ethical manner. Communication needs to open at every level so that small fires can be extinguished before they burn down an entire company.

Here's what went wrong at Volkswagen?
NBJ November 2015

Volkswagen is in the midst of one of the largest business scandals of all time. Surely there's something leaders can learn from the brand's disastrous mistake of trying to cover up emissions fraud in their cars. Whether you're an international car manufacturer, a politician or a mom-and-pop shop, experience has shown that deceit never works in business. Truth and transparency is the only response that can help you win in the end.

The scandal: Recent investigations into diesel-powered Volkswagen models found that the vehicles tested for emissions each carried a "defeat device" that falsely showed emissions meeting standards. The testing covered 11 million cars manufactured and sold by Volkswagen worldwide, including 500,000 in the United States, over the last six years.

Unfortunately, rather than owning up to the error early on, the formerly trusted brand insisted that emissions results and subsequent investigations in more than two-dozen countries were only related to "technical issues" that Volkswagen could soon resolve.

The public saw through the ruse. In the last 10 days of September the company lost more than a third of the market value of its stock and continues to trade near its low point. Not long after the scandal came to light the CEO left the company. More recently, several engineers who supposedly did the dirty work of building the "defeat device" are being individually targeted and blamed for the gaffe. Sadly, one of the largest manufacturers in the world has been ripped part by an *avoidable* scandal.

The issue: By allowing its engineers to systematically cheat the emissions industry, one can only conclude that Volkswagen must have suffered a massive cultural breakdown at the top. But why did they think they could get away with it? What voice told them that it was just fine to continue to cheat? The obvious conclusion is a gross lack of integrity, which as in most massive companies rests squarely on the shoulders of the CEO, board of directors and senior leadership.

Integrity starts at the top where VW leaders have the responsibility to practice doing the right things in every circumstance—in other words modeling the right behavior. In addition to demonstrating integrity, it's equally important for senior leaders throughout the organization to talk about and teach high standards at every opportunity.

The lessons: The first lesson we already know and would be naïve to ignore in the future: In business the bad guys all get caught. The second lesson is that integrity always starts at the top. It is the responsibility of senior leadership to both exemplify the right behavior and teach ethical standards. This is the key to total understanding and commitment in corporate culture.

If you are in a leadership role managing just a few people or even thousands you have an obligation to do the right thing and to encourage your people to do the same. It is essential to talk about standards of acceptable conduct regularly no matter how many times your team may have heard it before. Your goal is to ensure that everyone understands that there is no tolerance for a lack of ethics—ever—in your organization.

Let the Volkswagen scandal be a lesson in how *not* to act in business. Walk the high road.

7. DECISIONS

Leaders must push decision-making down the ladder
NBJ Sept 2014 (Originally "Push decision making down the ladder")

When decision-making is pushed to those truly accountable it takes the monkey off your back—and places it where it belongs. I learned this lesson early in my career and credit it as a significant cog in the wheel of success. When decision-making is made at the lowest possible level in the organization, ownership and pride follow. Your people are empowered, and you're free to think and lead.

Next time you feel pushed to make a decision, stop and ask yourself this question: Who is going to be accountable for the execution? If the answer is not you, then maybe the decision belongs to someone else. Don't jump to make decisions that could and should be made by others. Execution will usually work best when those accountable make the final decision.

Here's an example: During my Tractor Supply store visits salespeople often tell me about new product suggestions, usually based on what they've heard from customers. It would be easy for me to have the buyer test the new product, but then I would own it. The better solution is to pass along any reasonable new product idea to the proper buyer. The buyer then owns the decision and will quickly tout the new product as a wild success or quickly make sure a loser goes away. That is putting decision-making and accountability in the same place.

Likewise, sometimes operations decisions would be dropped in my lap, to which I responded, "Who is best positioned to make this decision?" The decision needs to go to those who have the most knowledge—and those are usually the people closest to the work. See, we're back to accountability. Those who will actually be responsible for getting the work done generally make the best decisions.

So next time an employee asks you what you think ought to be done about a particular issue, don't answer so fast. A smarter response might be to ask, "What do you think ought to be done?" In most cases that person would make a much better decision.

Part of your job as a leader is to identify when to push decision-making down the ladder so your mind is no longer clogged with unnecessary data. You should be free to think creatively. After all, your time and horsepower are best spent envisioning the future of your business.

You succeed when your team succeeds
NBJ May 2022

You can think of success as an equation: The success of individual team members adds up to the sum total productivity in your work group. Simply, when they are successful, you are successful. That means it's always in your best interest to help your people do the best possible job for the greater good. Here are a few pathways to success:

Support skill building: Self-improvement is human nature. Most of us are driven to consistently build and refine our skills. But as leaders in an organization, it's our responsibility to make sure people have the skills *to do the job*. That means constantly evaluating the best internal or third-party training processes and ensuring that coaching or mentoring happens at every turn.

Once basic operational skills are in place, forward-looking leaders will turn to skill building—developing talent who can move to higher levels of responsibility. In the long run, leaders earn respect and loyalty for their relentless efforts to build skills of the whole team.

Procure the right resources: It is hard to produce a finished product when parts are missing, the computer is down or instructions are unclear. I experienced this kind of frustration early in my career while managing busy checkout lines at a grocery store.

Our biggest service slowdowns—and frustrated customers—came when one of three things went missing: paper bags, receipt tape or change. You can guess what topics quickly made it to the top of my daily checklist.

As a leader, it's your job to make sure your team can do their job. Achieving planned results will only work if everyone has easy access to the right tools, supplies and resources for the production process to move smoothly.

Coach for success: Stay close to your team. Good leaders will spend a disproportionate amount of time coaching but also listening their people. Be available when your people want to talk and make them comfortable speaking to the boss. The hardest part? Really listening, which can be difficult for hard-charging leaders.

You will learn more from your team than anywhere else. I'm a believer that "those closest to the work know the most about it." Being in the daily mix will help you better understand the work, personalities and even special talents that can benefit your organization.

This is also an excellent time to gather process-improvement ideas. When you can hear—and see—suggestions in the field you may be able to respond more proactively, constructively and graciously, whether the idea is adopted or not. Listening early can often identify problems when they are minor, allowing for quicker, less costly course correction.

One of the most powerful organizational cultures is "servant leadership," or providing the support that *every individual* needs to be successful. Leaders are always under pressure to complete tasks, but the most successful leaders can balance deliverables with duty—developing the talent of everyone on their team.

Hiring is your most important decision
NBJ July 2016

A leader's biggest, best and most important decisions typically involve people. The impact of a "people decision" is unparalleled because it can have an enormous trickled-down influence on a company. Since these profound decisions involve complicated human beings, we don't always get them right. We, too, are only human. In fact, I can remember a few bonehead moves I made right alongside those solid people choices that changed the course of Tractor Supply, along with my own career.

The short of it is, people matter in business. Despite all the amazing benefits that automation and technology bring, having the right people on board will not only define your organization, but also your role as a leader as you help select those key employees. When you surround yourself with "stars," your life and your career can take off in new and sometimes unexpected ways. When your team is really competent, you'll have the luxury of being able "to see over the hill and around the corner," which is the ultimate goal of any senior trailblazer.

One of the best books ever written on this topic is "Who" by Geoff Smart and Randy Street. This classic occupies a cherished spot on my leadership shelf, and I continue to reference it when I have questions about the process—and power—of selecting great people. The best thing about the book is it very quickly gets to the heart of the issue: common mistakes leaders make during the selection process—from recruiting to interviewing. Like me, I suspect many of you will kick yourself over some of the everyday issues all leaders struggle with at some point when trying to make the smartest, most informed decisions about personnel.

This manual helped me stop detrimental practices in their tracks and get focused on finding workers who would truly thrive in the Tractor Supply retail environment. Among Smart and Street's in-depth recommendations are these timeless tips:

Hire "A" players: To do that leaders must first define expectations in clear, measurable terms instead of the typical generic job description. This may sound simple, but it takes a lot more effort than you'd think and is indispensable in the process of selecting effective team players.

Build your roster: One key chapter discusses the most efficient sourcing process for building your talent pool. Building a roster of quality candidates is essential to success. Intelligent background checks and initial screening can help you sort the wheat from the chaff quickly so you don't waste valuable time on those who don't measure up. If you're not talking to an "A" player, just move on.

Ask good questions: When interviewing, asking the right kind of queries is critical. Every leader can learn to interview better. It's just a matter of practicing how to ask the right questions, how to follow up, and how to read the actions and responses of your candidate. "Who" gives sound advice on the number of interviews, who should participate in the process and the timing of those interviews.

"Sell" the position: After you have made the most informed decision possible, you may still need to sell a top candidate on joining your organization. The book walks leaders through the entire sales process, from positioning the position to getting complete buy-in from the family.

If you have any doubts about the selection process, I urge you to spend some time with "Who." You can only get better by learning the trade secrets of selection and honing your skills to build the best team.

Be proactive in tackling difficult situations
NBJ February 2017

Leaders frequently face all sorts of difficult situations with team members, peers and bosses. Issues might include bad attitudes, performance shortfalls, procrastination, lack of communication, poor attendance or staff conflict, among other topics. As a leader it is your job to deal with these problems by keeping one goal in mind: a positive outcome.

Yet as compassionate human beings we tend to delay dealing with the obvious in hopes that all will somehow resolve itself. These issues often worry us and even keep us awake at night, but we tend to avoid facing them head on, soothing ourselves with thoughts like, "I won't worry, I know he will straighten out." How naïve we are.

The facts are that the sooner we deal with performance issues of any kind the more likely we will achieve a favorable outcome.

Procrastinating makes a problem that much more difficult to resolve. The best approach is to start planning as soon as you realize there is an issue and think the situation through clearly and carefully before taking action. Also, it's often helpful to discuss your plan with someone in human resources, or with your boss or maybe a mentor.

Here are a few key thoughts for planning your constructive discussion:

List the facts: Use actual performance-related figures and observations, such as: Job not completed as scheduled by 9 a.m. on Friday; absent this month on the 5th, 12th and 13th, totaling 17 days this year; on Tuesday, observed employee hollering at a coworker.

Avoid generalizations: Stay away from vague topics and generalizations. Don't criticize someone's attitude unless you have concrete examples and don't knock performance unless you have detailed, measurable data.

Plan ahead: Prepare your discussion points in advance so you are calm, cool and collected when you are ready to talk. Review these in detail and be sure you are armed with specifics in case others have questions. Don't react, but rather think before you respond to avoid saying things you will regret later.

Schedule the meeting: Set the discussion time few hours away, but don't provide enough time to sleep on it. Find a neutral location like a conference room. If talking in an office, set up so you're face to face and shut off all electronic devices that might interrupt a discussion.

Conduct yourself professionally: Ask for confirmation of the facts to avoid misunderstanding the issues. Stay composed and don't allow emotions to enter or take over the conversation. Then try to establish an agreed-upon future plan to put the issue to rest.

Difficult conversations are hard, but the longer we delay them the more difficult discussions will be. So as soon as you realize there's a conflict, take the initiative to resolve it early. Real leadership requires being proactive about performance issues.

THE CULTURE WARRIOR

Trust your instincts, even on big decisions
NBJ August 2020

Instincts begin to develop at an early age. If you trip and fall, you learn to look where you are going. As you learn to ride a bicycle your instincts kick in to keep you upright. Developing natural reactions to all sorts of things is part of growing up. We are continually learning how to react and then make decisions based on our experiences.

As adults we are called on to make all kinds of decisions using the knowledge and experience, we have accumulated. Most of these day-to-day decisions are simple and require no special work. But occasionally issues are more complex. Sometimes the facts lead us to one decision, but something inside says "Don't do it." That is what I call the conflict between apparent logic and your instincts, or natural intuition.

One of my mentors had a great approach to this conflict of interest: When all the facts lead to one decision but the hairs on the back of your neck stand up and tell you to do the opposite, listen to the hairs. In more simple terms, trust your instincts. Your lifetime of experience is speaking to you.

Instincts at work: When a salesperson is pitching a product, they typically talk about the features and benefits of this new gadget. We are told about product research, case uses, consumer ratings and so on. We digest all the good stuff we're told and then probably ask a few questions.

But at some point, it is time to make a decision—buy or don't buy. This is when our instincts might kick in. The facts say buy, but somewhere down deep we don't feel right making the purchase. My advice: Trust your intuition and move on. Decades of life experience are directing you. Listen.

Instincts come in to play during interviews, too. Getting the right candidates into the right positions can be critical to the future of an organization. That's a lot of pressure. But sometimes you need to go with your gut, because correcting a hiring mistake can be painfully consuming, disruptive and expensive. Not good.

I remember how I learned exactly this lesson. While screening an applicant who had an impressive resume, looked the part and interviewed well something just didn't seem right. Yet all the facts showed that this was the right person for the job. And after discussing the situation with an associate I made the decision to hire. Oops. It was not long before we realized that I had made big mistake. The employee had the right skills but was a cultural misfit. I should have followed my instincts.

Like personnel, there are other big decisions that make it tough to feel like you can go with your gut. For example, capital decisions like purchasing an office building or a factory have long-term implications and need deep due diligence. The same can be said of big software purchases that impact large parts of a company and its employees. Mistakes on purchases of this nature are far-reaching and very difficult to overcome.

The bigger the decisions the more time and effort needs to be applied. In this case, build a well-researched list of pros and cons. But when it comes time to say yes or no, trust your instincts. If a feeling has been nagging you from the start, it's probably the one you should pay attention to most.

We all accumulate a wealth of go-to knowledge over time. That is instinct, and it should not be ignored. When all is said and done, human intuition can be our greatest guide.

8. CULTURE

Company leaders responsible for corporate culture
NBJ April 2011

Leaders are always accountable for the culture in their own business unit. By nature, every organization has a corporate culture. And regardless of your title, if you are in a leadership role, it's an important part of your job to communicate and develop the essential elements of that culture.

By simply accepting responsibility and taking an active role in building a strong and positive culture, you can expand your influence in ways that lead to greater productivity and teamwork. Here are some ideas for getting started:

R-E-S-P-E-C-T: A positive and healthy business unit culture is built within an environment of respect. Start creating that atmosphere with simple deeds: Look people in the eye. Communicate clearly. Say "please" before requests and "thank you" after accomplishments. A respectful leader breeds a general culture of respect.

Be transparent: A constructive culture is one of openness on all key subjects. When you share strategic and tactical direction with your team members, they will be best positioned to help you achieve larger goals. When you share thoughts and concerns, others will be able to offer constructive ideas. On the other hand, if you operate by keeping secrets you run the risk of undermining productivity—and ultimately respect for you as a leader.

Listen diligently: Listening with intention is crucial to earning respect and creating a culture that attracts smart, motivated employees and encourages superior productivity. When leaders listen, team members follow suit, building morale and confidence throughout the business unit. If you don't listen you may lose respect of others while missing out on some very good ideas.

Recognize achievement: A culture of recognition spurs teamwork and productivity. When you recognize people for a job well done you will get more well-done jobs. Likewise, when you celebrate team success you will see further group achievement. Sincere recognition of any type is the most powerful motivator of people in the workplace.

Set the standard: As a leader you are tasked with setting the ethical standard for your work group. What you say and do every day become the cultural standard. If you bend the ethical rules—even a little—then your people will feel empowered to do the same. But if you are scrupulously principled in all your words and actions your team will likely follow your high moral example.

Regardless of their company size or position level, leaders set the tone in virtually all aspects of business. No matter what the culture of your organization you have an obligation as an individual leader to set a winning culture for your team.

Build a positive culture
NBJ March 2021

Let's say you and I operate competing hardware stores in the suburbs of the same city. Most likely we'd carry a similar assortment of products, arranged in a comparable store layout. And we'd probably be recruiting staff from the same labor pool.

One of us may have a slightly larger building or better location, but generally speaking we are in the same business. We certainly can't win a pricing war, so how does one of us gain a competitive advantage? The answer is culture.

Company culture is established one of two ways: Leadership drives it intentionally or it evolves on its own when leadership abdicates responsibility. The latter often leads to a negative and even toxic environment. On the other hand, when a company clearly defines its culture and constantly communicates its values, people generally come together. Teams tend to thrive and prosper in a culture of pro-active positivity.

How to build a better culture: CEOs have near complete authority to define culture in an organization. But few of us get to that level so we have to work with the existing company culture. But whether you are managing a team of 10 or 1,000 you can still impact attitudes in a positive way.

I learned early in my career that people tend to follow the boss's lead. If you are a quiet and stressed-out captain, most of your team will fall into the same mode. If your default is a smile and you appear happy, more often than not your team will follow suit.

In a leadership role you set the tone and, importantly, your actions as a leader define the culture in your unit. If you pad your expense reports or send out overly critical communications, you're setting a negative example. But when you display an upbeat attitude, you will soon find out how contagious it can be. Start here:

- Lead with a smile, a big "hello" and positive, intentional conversation.
- Start building a culture of earned respect through constructive, forward-looking performance evaluations.
- Carve out "coaching" time to send a message that you support, invest in and trust your team.

Your actions have a direct impact: Typically, a positive culture with high morale leads to more productivity and less turnover.

Make your message clear: Leaders build a positive culture by talking about it at every opportunity. Take most meetings and conversations as a chance to reiterate the mission and vision of your company. The goals for your business unit should also be part of regular discussions. Bottom line: No one should be confused or in the dark about mission, vision, values and goals. You'll maximize achievement by getting everyone on the same page.

Don't be shy about the topics that are central to culture. Remember, it's more than acceptable to talk about with your people about:

- The importance of ethical behavior
- Showing respect for others
- The impact of a positive attitude
- Helping peers, working as a team and taking initiative
- Embracing change and performance accountability for all

Regularly discussing—with as much enthusiasm as you can muster—all the factors that support a strong culture will keep the momentum alive.

I hope you already work for an organization with a positive culture, but if not, you still have the opportunity to build a strong culture in your environment. I hope you'll take the initiative to influence your work culture for the better.

Ethical values need to come from the top
NBJ July 2011

In light of recent big-company ethical meltdowns, I'd like to share something positive: a few highlights from the 30-year ethical history of Tractor Supply Company (TSC). Tom Hennesy—my mentor, boss and TSC's decade-plus CEO in the 80s—was very clear, very regularly, about ethics in our organization. He talked to new store managers about the importance of always telling the truth and standing behind our products as well as our individual actions. In conversations, meetings and writings he crystallized his position that there was simply no room for a lack of ethics *anywhere* in the corporation. And, perhaps most importantly, he said it a lot—like he meant it.

Doing the right thing: The topic of basic honesty became a bedrock principle of Tractor Supply Company. In fact, despite rapid expansion over 20 years, and the challenges that come along with communicating ethical principles company-wide, TSC took the time to put a moral code in writing. As the company formalized its Mission and Values (M&V), ethics became value No. 1. It reads: Do the "right thing" and always encourage others to do the right, honest and ethical things.

No-excuses customer service: Ethics extended easily to relationships. If a customer had an issue with a product, Tom taught us to say without excuses, "Mr. Smith, we are going do whatever it takes to make it right." And regarding customer service, he reiterated one simple point: You can never get in trouble for taking care of a customer. And no one ever did.

Relentless communication: Taking over the mission for honesty in everything, current CEO Jim Wright ably leads a consistent and newly focused push for ethical values in all company materials and communications: handbooks, pocket cards, newsletters, all sales meetings and at Tractor Supply University. And this isn't window dressing. When TSC employees meet new people, they often share M&V cards. And every "Tractor U" graduate can attest to restless—and passionate—senior executive talks about the importance of values.

Today, and during my 28-year tenure, there has never been a doubt about Tractor Supply Company values. When an organization's values agenda starts at the top, as it does at TSC, and is coupled with persistent communication, the potential for a massive ethical collapse is eradicated.

First secret of doing business: keep no secrets
NBJ March 2011

A "no secrets" approach to leadership offers tremendous benefit—and surprisingly little risk. Over the years, I have met and worked with business people who were reluctant to share more than "the basics" with employees. They all suffered from that "too much information" mentality—that somehow sharing too much might lead a competitor to uncover a big trade secret or more confusion among employees.

There are a variety of justifications for keeping workers—and even business partners—in the dark, but in my experience these are unfounded. Instead, it's this very secrecy that erodes productivity in organizations.

My longtime mentor and boss, a commensurate business philosopher and storyteller, believed sharing information with everyone was at the heart of a strong organization. People would do their best if they felt connected to a team that kept no secrets, he said, and this philosophy became a cornerstone of the Tractor Supply Company success story.

- **Trust building:** Sharing information goes a long way in building trust and loyalty in the business world. One clear demonstration of Tractor Supply Company's belief in gaining trust through transparency was its decade-long publication and distribution of an annual report—when the company was still private.
- **Job security:** Put yourself in the position of an employee who is either in the know or in the dark. When included, you feel like you genuinely belong and can contribute more than just labor. If you are left in the dark, you are more likely to feel insecure and suspicious, and may be recruited more easily to work for another company.
- **Good ideas:** In most businesses the best ideas come from those closest to the work. The more knowledge those people possess, the more productive their ideas. In my nearly 30 years visiting hundreds of Tractor Supply stores and talking with thousands of employees, I can say with sincerity that the best and most practical ideas about our products and processes came from the folks in the stores.
- **Employee engagement:** With no secrets about how and why a company does business, employees understand or are free to inquire about all aspects of the organization—sales, new products, trends, the direction of the company, etc. Likewise, in a no-secrets environment, leaders who share, ask good questions and

listen carefully can collect the best overall knowledge about the business.

Collaborative culture: When you share your business vision with employees and business partners, they can better grasp the value of their contribution. Employees who are included and valued can become engaged more productively, contribute more frequently and build loyalty more quickly.

So, remember, keep no secrets. Trust breeds trust. Trust your people and they will trust you and your organization as a whole.

The importance of trust in business
NBJ January 2015

Instinctively we all know that building a high level of trust is the right thing to do. However, can you really measure the impact of trust on business? Yes. I found this out after researching study after study that overwhelmingly validated the economic benefits of operating in a high-trust environment. The returns to shareholders have been measured at double, triple and even quadruple those of lower-trust organizations. Wherever you are on the organizational chart, there's ROI tied to trust.

Let's look at some of the key components of high-trust organizations:

- **Set focused direction:** Take measures to ensure everyone knows as clearly and completely as possible where the business is headed. Then consistently share goals and performance measures. For example, daily sales compared to plan is the most important measure for Tractor Supply Company stores. Every morning in every store the sales results are shared with the team.
- Success is possible only when the entire team can see the future and measure the past.

- ➢ **Function as a team:** Collaboration helps achieve goals more efficiently. Knocking down the silos or even preventing them from being erected in the first-place nurtures the right environment for teamwork to thrive. Leaders who empower team members see much greater levels of cooperation and transparency than those who hold back and micromanage.
- ➢ **Coach for success:** The difference between success and "wild success" is often the amount of time and effort leaders devote to the coaching process. In my retail world I spent inordinate time in stores with a wide variety of staff studying business operations from every angle. Big portions of those trips were spent coaching and teaching leaders at every level.
- ➢ **Make team decisions:** Ultimately leaders are accountable for big decisions, but they should be made with integral team consultation. Push decision-making down the ladder whenever possible. When team members are engaged in the process the likelihood of making a good decision is increased, as is the strength of support and execution.
- ➢ **Support the team:** Teams function best when they have all the tools needed to get the job done. Providing those tools is a leadership responsibility. Your team needs to know you are available for support and consultation. You are a key reference and resource, not a dictator. Engage, listen and empower your people for maximum results.
- ➢ **Celebrate success:** There is nothing that generates more confidence and team trust than achieving success and celebrating those special milestones in an appropriately motivating way.

The research is clear: Strong levels of trust yield strong results. Still doubting the importance of running a high-trust business? Just Google "organizational trust."

Respect is an integral part of leadership that must be earned
NBJ May 2011 (Original title "Respect: An Integral Part of Leadership")

True leaders are respected and admired people. They have the confidence to build strong teams and motivate others to achieve. Do you know how they get to this position? They earn it. You too will earn respect and admiration from your team by focusing on one simple yet effective karmic approach: showing respect for those around you.

Get personal: Get to know a little about your teammates and show some genuine interest in their lives. Basic mutual respect is as simple as starting each day with a thoughtful "good morning" and maybe a few words of a personal nature. Interpersonal inquires like "How did Johnny do in his ball game yesterday?" or "How is your mother recovering from her knee surgery?" go a long way in earning respect from the people you lead. Never underestimate the impact of the personal touch in building real team spirit.

Always engage: We always have to get down to the business of business—and this is a perfect opportunity to earn greater respect from your team. Before you pass out assignments, take just a few minutes to engage your team around the business plan and objectives. Ask for comments and have a lively discussion. One individual idea can really make a difference—and then the whole team wins. When people are involved on the front end of a project, they will more clearly understand goals and objectives. And when a team is engaged early on you often see a stronger sense of commitment and achieve better results in the end.

Common courtesy: What may sound like common sense is often ignored in the business world. The shortest way to earning respect is by *regularly* using three little respect-building words: "please" and "thank you." Tacking on please to any request—large or small—quickly gives the tone of the conversation a positive spin. When a task is completed, a hearty "thank you" goes a long way in the eyes of your team.

Pay attention: Another simple but powerful respect builder: Pay attention when people try to talk to you. In today's environment of instant, 24/7 communication, focusing is easier said than done. It takes a strong commitment on your part to really concentrate on each visitor, but you earn deep respect when you give others your full attention. Shut off the phone, physically move away from your computer (or at least ignore it), look your visitor in the eye and really listen.

To be effective, leaders need followers. When you show sincere interest in your people, they will gain respect for your leadership. When you demonstrate courtesy and compassion you will earn their admiration. It's not that complicated: Treat others with respect and in turn they will respect you.

Recognition is the no. 1 motivator
NBJ December 2019

My predecessor and mentor at Tractor Supply preached the impact of sincerely recognizing the efforts of all employees. Over time, acknowledgement became a way of life for us. And today it is one of the key foundations of the company culture.

When you think about the happiest moments in your life, I'll bet many of them relate to someone recognizing something you did well. The simple process of sharing a little gratitude for good work doesn't take much time—and generally yields measurable benefit.

Making regular and sincere recognition part of your daily routine can lead to a healthier, happier culture. In that environment things typically get done better, on time and on budget. And it will certainly help you earn the respect and admiration of your team and your associates. Here are some ways to start a recognition practice at your organization:

- ➢ **Make it a habit:** During the workday start recognizing performance as often as you can with simple gestures like a positive pat on the back. At day's end, a sincere "nice work today, Joe" goes along way.

- ➢ **Keep it sincere:** One word of caution about recognition: Always be honest and sincere. Make sure your recognition is for real accomplishment that is well understood by all. False or fake praise can boomerang on you.
- ➢ **Talk it up:** When your team achieves a new goal, it's time to share the good news. Gather your crew, remind them about what they've accomplished and then high-five it all around. Never wait to celebrate accomplishments.
- ➢ **Write a note:** A thoughtful handwritten note shows that you took an extra moment to recognize the impact of a great performance. Your people will cherish such notes and may keep them for a long time. I have two boxes of personal notes I received over the years!
- ➢ **Send it home:** Whether it's a simple note or corporate award, try sending it home. Acknowledgements from work that arrive on a doorstep get special attention from family, which can help build stronger bonds between work and family life.
- ➢ **Celebrate big successes:** When the group accomplishes a larger, long-term goal, it's time to celebrate. It could be a pizza dinner, maybe some time off or a visit from a senior executive. Do whatever it takes to make your people feel good about coming back to work every day.
- ➢ **Present awards:** Formal awards at company meetings can do wonders for team morale. You can celebrate with plaques, gifts, even trips—whatever makes sense for your culture. Being a little unpredictable with awards can make this approach even more exciting.
- ➢ **Find a signature "smile":** My personal trademark for recognition is giving "smiley faces," in the form of stickers or an emoji on an email. I learned this trick from my wife a long time ago. It sounds silly, but it works. People can't help but light up when they see a smile. It's just a different form of appreciation.

We generally think of a boss recognizing an employee, but acknowledgement can work in other ways. In a team, anyone can pat someone else on the back for an accomplishment. Individuals will likely gain some additional respect, and morale might get a little better, too. There's no downside. You can also give your boss a little credit. Just be careful not to overdo it.

However, it plays out, practicing regular recognition for good performance helps to build a strong company culture. If you pat me on the back for good work today, the odds are that tomorrow I may try to do even better. As a leader, this sure sounds like a winning formula.

Whether it's a yes or no, responding earns respect

NBJ November 2016. (Original title: Responding earns respect)

When you take the time to make a personal call and leave a message, you expect to receive a response in a reasonable amount of time. The same principle applies to personal letters and emails. No one wants to be in the position of having to abandon an initiative or handle that uncomfortable follow-up communication. Likewise, no recipient is simply too busy or too special not to reply with even the shortest response or resolution. It's a matter of respect.

One helpful scenario is to put yourself in the position of a salesperson continually looking for new prospects. Every day you are making contacts with the hope of closing a sale. A "yes" is a sale—you achieved your goal. A "no" isn't exactly good news, but you can respect a quick, clear, forthright decision and move on to the next prospect. But what about that buyer who never even acknowledged your effort or attempt to communicate? For many, that's worse than a "no." Conclusion: You're thrilled with the buyer that says "yes," respect the buyer that says "no" and hold very little esteem for the buyer who ignored you.

Now let's say you are planning a big party at your house and you send 50 invitations. Twenty couples respond that they will be attending and 10 couples decline. Now you know for sure you need to plan for 20 couples, but what about the other 20? If they all show up the party will double in size. So how much food should you prepare? How much wine should you buy? Should you call the ones who did not respond? It is a quandary for the host. Obviously, the polite thing to do is to respond promptly one way or the other.

Courtesy is no different in the professional world. I remember an incident when Walmart opened a farm store in Kirksville, Missouri, which created real sense of concern for my company, Tractor Supply. I took the initiative to call CEO David Glass who could have easily ignored me—just a guy running a small chain of farm stores—but he chose the opposite path. He answered his phone personally and invited me to Bentonville to talk about retailing. Our meeting helped put us on a mutually beneficial path that led to Tractor Supply eventually leasing hundreds of vacant Walmart stores. We later took over their farm store. Responding paid off for both organizations.

The next time someone requests something of you, spend the few seconds (or minutes) to provide a polite response. If the request is from a salesperson, a simple "no" allows that person to move on quickly. RSVP-ing to a party invitation allows the host to plan on the right amount of food. Answering to an employee needing a little advice might make the worker's job easier—and yours. Responding to requests is simple courtesy, and ignoring someone's communication will only undermine your reputation as a leader.

When a request comes your way, consider the time and courage it took to the person to prepare and send such communication. Doesn't it deserve a response? Each thoughtful and direct reply will move a leader one rung higher on the scale of respect.

What businesses can learn from government mistakes
NBJ April 2012

Two recent high-profile incidents have proven there's a lack of basic leadership at the highest levels of government. The first involved Government Services Administration (GSA) members partying in grand style all over the U.S. The second was the Secret Service prostitute scandal before the hemispheric conference in Columbia. Both examples show a blatant disregard for basic leadership by chief executives in some of our top agencies.

Unbelievably unethical: The GSA left a trail of over-the-top carousing from Hawaii to Las Vegas while a nation in debt continued to fall further behind every day. There's no excuse: While the GSA leader did not even attend the infamous near-million-dollar Vegas conference, she certainly still had oversight responsibility. Taxpayers (the employers) expect the GSA to fulfill its mission of maintaining government buildings and related services at a reasonable cost. We don't expect to be supporting our leaders' wild nights on the Strip.

The case of the Secret Service demonstrates an even greater lack of leadership. If the Secret Service director had regularly communicated a culture of ethical behavior and shown a passion for the integrity of the organization, it is unlikely that any Secret Service member would have ever considered hiring a hooker on a presidential mission. Even if one agent got out of line, you'd expect others to jump in to either correct the situation or turn in the offender. Sadly, devoid of ethical leadership, these entitled agents felt no sense of responsibility to themselves, the agency, the President or the public.

Learning our lessons: Similar issues raise their ugly heads all the time in the business world. There are stories daily about value breakdowns by corporate leaders who have failed to set the right ethical direction. Instead of endless investigations into why these situations occur and irrelevant laws to prevent them from happening again, the action we should take to prevent ethical lapses is re-instituting basic leadership principles for chief executives. Here's a little refresher on Leadership 101:

- Be clear about values and never bend those values.
- Passionately discuss values so everyone, without exception, is on the same page.
- Set clear direction and expectations that will lead to achieving the expected results.

- Define the central mission clearly, loudly and repetitively so that no one is confused.
- To be sure your message sticks, say it 10 times or more since people only retain 10% of what they hear a week later.
- Communicate regularly so people can understand and follow your mission going forward.

Strong, ethical leaders are the foundation of good government and back-to-basics business. It's up to each leader to start changing our world one principle at a time.

General Motors recalls reflect a defective culture
NBJ July 2014

General Motors is currently recalling more vehicles than it sold in the last eight years. The number of vehicles recalled is 29 million and counting. This is an amazing statistic, and the recall seems to affect multiple models across all of the GM brands. That means that anyone who owns a GM car or truck is likely to be on a recall list.

The financial cost of this debacle, according to GM, was $1.3 billion during the first quarter of this year and $1.2 billion in the second, and outside professionals estimate the total cost could top a whopping $7 billion dollars! The damage to the company's reputation is incalculable, and the human cost is unforgivable. The actual number of people killed or injured is not yet clear, and it's impossible to measure the degree of personal loss for the families and communities who trusted GM with their lives.

How could something this monstrous actually happen?

Anyone who pays attention to the news knows that much of this problem revolves around a defective ignition switch, but the real reason is even more frightening, because all of it could have been prevented.

The root cause is a culture that fueled a dysfunctional environment. Poor leadership, lack of communication, and selective listening made the GM culture far more defective than the single flawed part that was discovered, ignored, and left unchecked. It took nearly a decade to acknowledge and implement a simple recall that could have saved an (as of yet) undetermined number of lives.

Every company has a culture, and the strongest of those cultures are intentionally driven by senior leadership. Top executives set the tone for every organization, and from that deliberate direction a distinct way of doing business emerges. When the leaders regularly talk about the values and the mission of the company, employees and front-line managers listen and fall in line. When senior leaders talk openly about ethics and practice what they preach, their organizations will follow.

On the other hand, when employees are criticized for delivering bad news or are ignored when they make unpopular recommendations, they tend to avoid tough decisions, follow the easiest course of action (or inaction), and choose the lowest-cost (or no-cost) option in order to protect themselves. When bosses only want to hear good news, important information is inevitably suppressed. And when employees become more concerned with their status and career safety than with the safety of whatever they are producing and selling, bad things happen.

The ignition switch issue stems from a culture that does not discuss and, as a result, does not value integrity. When I ran Tractor Supply Company, we discovered that the best way to make integrity and ethical action a priority was to talk about it. Discussing the importance of "doing the right thing" is a central responsibility of every front-line manager and is an integral part of the company culture.

A well-run organization encourages the reporting of important issues and rewards workers who help solve problems. Well-run organizations celebrate the discovery of potentially dangerous or damaging long-term issues and publicize those findings throughout the company to encourage others to speak up.

It's tough to overstate the importance of setting a high ethical bar and maintaining an open, "no secrets" work environment. The situation at GM should be seen as a lesson to top executives across all industries. Business leaders have a moral obligation to lead with clear, solid, and regular communication, not only about the vision for the future, but also about current and essential organizational values.

Ethical leadership is everything—whether in business, in politics, or in life. Those who walk the high road will win in the long term regardless of the many bumps along the way. While it is pretty clear that GM's issues didn't develop overnight and have likely been growing for decades, it is also clear that in the long run, a breakdown in the culture of integrity will inevitably catch up with any of us who ignore our moral obligation to our employees, our shareholders, and—most importantly—our customers.

You can't talk enough about your company values
NBJ September 2017

Teaching kids' basic values is arguably a parent's most important job. We repeat these important messages constantly but wonder, "Will they ever listen?" In the long run, they do. And we can only hope that children will put these core values to use in their professional lives.

Why? Because the practice of maintaining solid values is as essential to success in business as it is everywhere in life.

As both a parent and a life-long leader, I've made values a big part of my message. At Tractor Supply sales meetings I always found time to talk about our company values. I hammered on this so much that one corporate event several senior managers asked kiddingly if I was going to get up on stage and talk about what I *always* talk about. My response: "Damn right!" Leaders can never say enough about values.

As business leaders we have the responsibility to reinforce the basic values of our organization with those who work for us. Instilling the right values in a team can have a huge impact on the results we produce. We should never underestimate the impact of continually communicating the values that are so important in building true teamwork.

Here are some values that pertain to every business:

Respect: is an essential component for ensuring that teams not only get along, but also achieve results and long-term success. Sometimes people under pressure can get very emotional about hitting difficult goals, and occasionally individuals just "lose it." When tempers flare leaders must step in to calm things down and encourage peacemaking. It's our obligation to talk about the importance of maintaining mutual respect as a principle for success.

Ethical behavior: should be basic practice in all business operations and in all aspects of our lives. Your team needs to know about your organization's ethical standards and hear about them repeatedly from you. It's also essential that leaders are available and open to discuss ethical dilemmas that may present themselves unexpectedly. It's important to demonstrate and voice your commitment to ethical behavior as well as your openness to coaching on the subject.

Communication: that is open and honest is another fundamental value in every organization. Hidden or concealed information, whether intentional or not, creates a lack of trust that can lead to mistakes, misunderstandings and bad decisions. As leaders we need to demonstrate open communication in all we do and never keep secrets from our team. The great leaders practice free and open communication as a way of life and talk about its importance on a regular basis.

Initiative: is another value that every leader wants in a team. Start by letting your people see you take the initiative on a project and then discuss how and why you did it. Challenge your folks to do the same. And when a team member actually takes the initiative on a new project coach him or her along the way. When you see a big success, make a big deal of it. Celebrate initiative and you will get more of it in return.

Positive attitudes: will encourage teams to work together enthusiastically. As leaders we set the tone—and people tend to mimic our behavior. Be positive and upbeat, and your team will typically follow your lead.

Values matter everywhere in life. So, no matter the time or place, demonstrate your passion for values by setting the right example. Then find the time to talk about your principles more frequently than you think you should. Values really do matter.

9. TALENT

Talent development is the path to success
NBJ May 2021

Our effectiveness as leaders hinges on the people we are willing to develop. One of the keys to the success of any organization is how its managers select and mentor top talent. When you surround yourself with a high-quality, well-trained team you significantly increase your odds of winning at work.

And when you commit to prioritizing talent development you can bet that senior leaders will take note of your efforts. As you assess your career, be sure to move procuring a circle of good people to the top of your important goals. I guarantee that a track record of talent development will make a big difference in your long-term success. Take it step-by-step:

1. Perform a serious, written assessment of your team and, where helpful, enlist your human resources department for support.
2. Pinpoint your "high-potential" people and map a development plan for each. And don't overlook those who may appear a little shy—sometimes real talent is just below the surface.
3. Provide opportunities for your most promising people to attend the right classes, explore educational experiences, tackle the toughest challenges and learn from an executive mentor.
4. Then follow your key people carefully to help them achieve maximum success, because ultimately their long-term success contributes to yours.

Finding, securing and building top talent: No matter where you are always be scouting for talent that could benefit your organization. When you meet new people, engage and ask questions. Be on the lookout at industry events, within your company, even at community or social events. Who knows where an exceptional person could enter your life?

In the process you might also run across candidates who would be good fits for other functions in your organization. Even if you don't have a current opening, make a note of good prospects, because you never know when the need may arise.

Once you have identified a candidate who matches an open position, initiate a conversation, explain your organization and then schedule an interview. Conducting an effective interview is no easy task and is a skill that even the best leaders are forever refining. Take your time, plan your questions carefully and give your candidate plenty of time to respond—sometimes "ramblings" can tell you more than you get from the questions alone.

If things look promising schedule a second interview and ask another key person to join you. Another opinion can provide important perspective. If you want to build your interviewing skills further, I suggest the book "Who" by Geoff Smart.

When you hire a new person, go out of your way to plan the first few days and weeks for maximum success. Start with an orientation of the organization, along with assigning a "buddy" for the first few weeks. The goal is to get your new hire comfortable and productive as quickly as you can.

Knowing how to develop talent will set you apart from your peers and will garner respect in your organization. When senior leaders assess their executives and managers, measures always relate to people—morale in the unit, personnel turnover and the development of future talent. When you are seen as a builder of your company's next generation, you are positioning yourself for the next step up the ladder.

Want to get ahead? Be a talent developer!

Invest in your best people
December 2021

As a business leader you know that you are judged by your results. But it's always the people that make the biggest difference in getting the job done.

Suppose you're in a leadership role running a good-sized department with a couple dozen employees when a new assignment drops in your lap. The boss wants you to implement a program affecting several departments, which involves significant procedural and operating changes that will impact many employees.

What do you do?

Your challenge is this: You can delegate the assignment to a key team member or you can work around the clock to do it yourself. Looking at your team, if you can quickly say, "I have the person to get the job done," give yourself a big pat on the back. If you don't have those go-tos, maybe it's time to examine what you should have done—and will do in the future—to develop the best people for your team.

Developing talent: the power of good people: Most high-growth companies invest heavily in the leadership development and hold key people accountable for that process. Why? Because they've learned that, more than anything else, it's quality people that make the biggest difference in an organization's level of success.

At Tractor Supply Company, for example, we evaluated district managers partly on how well they could develop store managers. Look at it this way: If you are a net exporter of store managers to other districts you are on a solid career path. Organizations always appreciate folks who can develop talent.

So how do you do that? One way is to assign difficult tasks to your best people so they can gain experiences that will lead to greater responsibility. Collaborate on big-picture goals but then step aside—you want team members to figure it out themselves like you probably did at first. When your best people really "own" a project, they will find creative ways to overcome obstacles to achieve success.

Your investment in developing your crew will always pay off. And your ROI will be greatest when you spend time with the people who are the most engaged, enthusiastic, and committed to the company and its mission.

Teaching and coaching build your organizations' ability to achieve results and, equally important, build morale. Over time, high morale translates to high productivity and low turnover. It's a long-term investment that will also lead to your greatest opportunity for personal growth.

Nurturing your leaders is a foundation of success
NBJ May 2012 (Original title: Leadership Development)

Qualifying and nurturing your next leaders: The success of Tractor Supply Company comes down to two big, complementary factors: a passionate customer-centric business strategy and a nurturing culture dedicated to people and ethics.

The first is a simple yet powerful approach that focuses all efforts on satisfying the needs of the real Tractor Supply customer: hobby farmers and others who live the unique rural lifestyle. This strategy has impacted everything from store locations, operating hours and merchandise to staff choices and marketing efforts.

The second equally important success factor is building a culture focused on nurturing people and always doing the right thing. This global corporate commitment to ethics and employee development requires respect and support for every team member. Leveraging a strong core value structure with unwavering integrity has translated to Tractor Supply's fanatical passion for providing the best customer service in America.

With over 1,100 locations, the key to success is simply the quality of the leadership at each Tractor Supply store. When leadership is competent and stable, the work day goes smoothly, employee turnover is low, customer relations are positive, inventories are well managed—and sales go up.

Raising standards: Building this type of culture depends almost entirely on selecting and developing the right leadership team. With standards this high it's not easy for people to secure a position with Tractor Supply and the interview process may take longer. But we learned a long time ago that the more time and effort we put into the talent selection process, the fewer issues we had to deal with later on.

Fostering talent: Once you have top-quality people on board, the next step is to build their skill bases so they can deliver first-class performance. Tractor Supply has outstanding programs for all leadership levels: store manager and other first-line supervisors; district manager and similar management positions; and executive leadership. Leadership classes carefully cover culture, values and mission, and many are taught by the company's most senior executives.

Never compromising: At our leadership institute we hear two common reasons for postponing leadership development: money and time constraints. The first excuse is "Times are tough—we can't afford it." The fact is, if you see a positive future for your organization, you can't afford *not* to develop your people. In tough times, cutbacks can be made in other areas of the organization, but never in creating the right leadership team. When circumstances improve, you'll be positioned to outgun your competitor, and your leadership will be prepared to take your company to the next level.

The second excuse is "We are just too busy." If you are actually too busy you need leadership education more than you think. If you feel overwhelmed you probably need more leadership help so you can learn how to manage that growth.

Bottom line: Compromising on the development of your team can actually compromise the future of your organization. In the long run, people are always the most important component in long-term success.

Share your leadership skills by taking the initiative to coach others
NBJ October 2014 (Orig. Taking the initiative to coach)

Got more than a few years in a business leadership role? You'd probably make a great coach. Think about it: You have been learning throughout your career, and much of that acquired knowledge could help others. Young folks need coaches, and coaching just feels great. In my five decades in leadership, I'm most proud of the time I spent coaching others. In fact, I count my key career accomplishment the development of others.

Don't shy away from a pivotal opportunity to apply your leadership skills in a new way. Here are a few ways that you can start to make an impact as a coach.

Ask questions: Start coaching by asking your first student some open-ended questions to gain key insight: What parts of your job do you most like? What do you find most challenging? So that you both get going in the right direction, ask for more detail, dig deep to understand your student and make a list of confidential issues you can help your student work on.

Share experiences: That means the good and the bad ones. This kind of honesty will help developing leaders learn and grow. Think of every story as an opportunity to teach. A personal success story about how you learned the ropes can motivate a young person to build his or her own path to success. Explanations of your challenges along the way are also a way to connect and help students avoid the same pitfalls.

Keep it real: Not only can you talk about your career and how you moved up the ladder from one position to another, you can also share conflicts you encountered with people. Realism, especially when it comes to business relationships, helps young folks grow. Ambitious young leaders have an almost unquenchable thirst for knowledge about how to get ahead—and your stories of navigating real relationships will help paint a picture for real growth.

Encourage networking: Since networking is so important to growth, explain how you've networked and talk about the relationships you've developed throughout your career. Include your student at lunch meetings with business people who could become part of his or her own network. Start demonstrating how networking is the path to professional—and personal—growth.

Here's how to coach others for success
NBJ November 2019

More than any other factor, the quality of our team will define us as leaders. To be successful we must spend an inordinate amount of time building and developing our employees. And coaching is the only way to do it right. Personal coaching is one of the most intimate and impactful components of team development.

To that end, it's important to schedule your coaching: Make it a top priority every day. Put it on your calendar. Don't let a crisis set you back. In the long run you will achieve the best result when you have the best team. And guess what? You are the person best positioned to build the individual competence of every member of your team.

To start, build a plan. Analyze the skills of each of your direct reports. Then decide where you would like to place the most emphasis. Big issues, obviously, will take the most time. But some coaching tips only take a couple of minutes. Plan your coaching time accordingly and maximize it. It may be your most important contribution.

Here are some more sound coaching tactics:

Attitude: Often when you hear about or observe someone with a bad attitude the real issue is something else entirely: a lack of awareness. Attitude issues seldom get better when left unattended. So don't procrastinate. Have a direct discussion using specific examples. When confronted with facts, many people admit that they did not realize the impact their words and actions were having on people and the workplace environment. That clarity is good foundation to build on.

Recognition: You have probably heard something along the lines of "recognition is the No. 1 motivator." While recognizing achievements or positive actions only takes only a little coaching it can be a big contributor to positive morale. A three-minute conversation can teach employees about the importance of patting other team members on the back. And it can have real impact.

Public speaking: Most people are fearful of standing in front of a group. Yet senior executives know that it is one of the most pivotal skills in business. Coaching public speaking takes time, patience and a lot of repetition. But in the long run it may be some of the most rewarding coaching you will ever do. A wise friend once told me, "Public speaking is like any other skill in life—the more you do it the better do it."

Networking: Many people are shy about reaching out to network with others, particularly those outside the company. But it's critical. I have seen so many business leaders grow exponentially once they learned to fly from a comfortable work nest. As a leader, it's your job to coach about the enormous benefit that comes from meeting different people. Talk about the entire networking process, build a repertoire of conversational questions and regularly suggest fresh contacts.

Difficult conversations: It is human nature to put off challenging conversations as long as possible. But we all know that in most cases the longer we procrastinate the more severe the situation. Leadership coaching on this topic is essential in many situations. Demonstrate and teach your people how to plan the conversation carefully, stick to the facts and avoid emotion to get through the toughest conversations.

Personnel selection: This is another scary topic for many people and one where our hand as a seasoned leader can help others make solid decisions. Challenge your people to ask the most insightful questions, which will likely lead to better decisions and hopefully avoid a hiring error that has to be addressed later on.

Leaders who work diligently to build team skills will soon witness confidence growth in individuals—often way beyond expectations. When a team is skilled and self-assured, everything runs better. And at that point leaders can get out of the weeds and spend more time looking to the future.

Many of the most rewarding moments in my career were when my coaching efforts blossomed. In the long run your fondest leadership memories will be about the people you helped develop.

Unlock your potential by spending time with the right people
NBJ—July 2011

Time is our most important business commodity. So, who you spend it with can make all the difference in your level of growth and accomplishment.

Planning each week is difficult, but effective time management is essential to personal growth and the effectiveness of your business unit. Start by analyzing how you've allocated your time over the last couple of months. In retrospect, you may find that you would have spent some part of it differently.

There is only so much time, and you can use it wisely by spending time with constituencies that are most important to accomplishing your goals. For example, allocating time with peers can help you benchmark yourself and your business operation. And you can really upgrade your skills by spending quality time with those in higher-level roles in your company and the community.

Employee interaction: In most business roles, time spent with your employees ranks at the top of the list. Your team generally knows the most about the work and can alert you to potential issues early in the process. Your people also typically have regular customer contact that can be invaluable in building your business. Listening, discussing and asking the right questions can give you key insight into your operation, and this knowledge can help you lead your team in the best possible direction.

Customer communication: There's no downside to staying close to customers. So, try to schedule the maximum amount of time with the customers who are important today—and particularly with those who are most likely to provide long-term growth. Take every opportunity to spend time with customers on their turf so you can best see how your product or service fits your customers' needs. And don't avoid those "difficult" customers who ask really tough questions. That eye-opening type of engagement can lead you to thinking about your business in different, and often more creative, ways. Regular and effective customer communication will reinforce a strong customer bond.

Partner potential: Strategic business partners, who provide various types of support for our operations, can make all the difference in our success. It's important to build time into your schedule for these critical alliances. Spending time with partners, particularly at their business locations, can help solve problems while they are still small—and can facilitate tactical planning for future growth. By putting in real face time, it is not uncommon to discover that business partners have additional capabilities that could contribute to the future success of your organization.

Common sense and effective leadership go hand in hand
NBJ June 2013

Leadership is not complicated. First, we need to work smart, and then we can go on to working hard. Working smart begins with a liberal application of common sense, so let's look at a few basic practices of people who lead effectively:

Set direction: Everyone wants to know where the ship is headed, so don't keep it a secret. Explain as much as you can and more often than you think necessary. Repetition is important. Experts say people remember only a small portion of what they hear, so repeating the message is essential to building a clear understanding your business-unit goals.

Support: Achievement takes place when people have the tools to get the job done. Your leadership role includes ensuring the right tools are close at hand and knocking down any obstacles that might get in way of productivity.

Engage: Everyone wants to be part of something, so engage your people as much as you can. When team members participate in the planning process, they will more clearly understand direction, plus they will be well positioned to make suggestions that could have a positive impact on the level of accomplishment.

Coach: The time you spend coaching and teaching pays off by multiplying productivity and reducing big, costly errors. You also earn the respect of your people. Perhaps most importantly, when you look back on your career, the highlights will most likely be the people you coached along the way.

Reward: When you teach your dog to do something you reward that behavior with a treat. People react the same way, except the treat is a pat on the back. It only takes a few seconds to acknowledge someone, so if you want more productive people, recognize those who achieve. Remember, recognition is still the No. 1 motivator.

Set the example: Model the behavior you expect from your team. If you want frugality, demonstrate it in all you do. If you expect team members to respect each other, go out of your way to show respect to every individual.

As you develop your leadership skills, let common sense be your guide. And that includes never letting your leadership position go to your head. Inflated egos have brought down more leaders than any other shortcoming. Be a common-sense leader.

Building on the basics is good for business
NBJ September 2012

There's no two ways about it: Business always comes down to economics. As a business leader you are in an ideal position to teach associates, employees, friends, family, and particularly children, about what makes our economic system—and our great nation—tick. In the process, you might just inspire the next generation of business superstars.

The United States achieved success through innovation, drive, passion and freedom. Don't be shy: Teach others about the forces that create jobs and wealth—and make our country great. Start lively discussions about the basic economics that have made the United States the envy of the world. This is your chance to be a leader, a listener, a coach and a teacher.

As a former CEO, I always start basic economics discussions by dispelling what I believe to be some serious misinformation in the marketplace. Here are some points that always seem to come up:

1. **Profit:** When a company makes a profit, it can reinvest in the business. Profit enables the enterprise to invest in facilities, equipment and people that will ultimately yield growth.
2. **Competition:** The nature of business is to grow revenue by outperforming the competition. When each company is challenged to outdo the next, creative ideas pop to the surface, resulting in better products and services often at lower costs. The best companies grow. The mediocre companies may survive. And the weak ones go away.
3. **Growth:** Growth means everyone's happy. Customers are buying more. Employees are more likely to have long-term security and increased compensation. Business partners who supply products and services to the enterprise do well. And stockholders see increased wealth.
4. **Bankruptcy:** The cream of the crop rises to the top. When weak companies are sold or liquidated, that's just part of the constant "cleansing" process that makes our economy vibrant. Assets are redeployed to make profits elsewhere.
5. **Monopoly:** When there is only one provider of a product or service, there's no incentive to be great. Innovation dies, service is typically poor and prices go up.
6. **Regulation:** The government's role is to see that the playing field is level and that generally accepted business and cultural norms are in play. However, growth slows when excessive regulations interfere with a business's day-to-day ability to operate.
7. **Policy:** Big long-term business investments include the evaluation of government policy. Predictability is key. If business is unsure about future taxes, environmental rules and trade regulations, business is less likely to make the big investments.

8. **Crony capitalism:** Any time business and government "get into bed with each other," watch out. Very often the outcome stifles competition and upsets the natural force of the market.
9. **Taxes:** The government collects money from citizens and businesses to redistribute for various reasons. But the real wealth and job creation comes from the private sector.

These are my nine economic basics. You'll likely have your own. However, you lead the discussion on economics, this is your opportunity as a business leader to initiate, educate and inspire. I leave you with this simple challenge: Be a teacher.

Joe Scarlett is the retired CEO of Tractor Supply Company
For more on leadership, see joescarlett.com
Or write Joe at Joe@joescarlett.com

Follow these 7 tips for better performance reviews
NBJ April 2018

Dread annual performance reviews? Most people do. Anxious employees may wonder if they're performing up to par. Executives worry whether they made the grade or provided enough guidance to teams. But without mandated measurements like performance reviews, employees, leaders and organizations can't improve and move forward.

So instead of fearing those performance reviews, let's try changing perspective. As one human resources executive put it perfectly: "Feedback is the breakfast of champions."

Remember, a leader's job is to coach and develop people. But how can an employee grow with no benchmarks or systems to measure progress? Feedback is an essential component for nurturing natural talent, and the performance review is the formal vehicle for that feedback.

They're not going away anytime soon, but let's can define some ways to reduce the stress level a little when it comes to performance reviews:

1. **Measurements:** If you can't measure performance, evaluations become very difficult. Measuring requires having predetermined objectives and clear goals to gauge against. For example, each fall Tractor Supply store managers work with district managers to establish reasonably attainable sales and profit goals for the following year. Team development and personal improvement goals are set at the same time. Whether professional or personal, every goal is measurable.
2. **Consistency:** Try not to drastically change how you benchmark your team members. While you may tweak some evaluation parameters over time, pulling the rug out from under an employee will undermine trust. Having an effective review template and consistent check-ins will help manage expectations and avoid any "surprises" on either side of the evaluation.
3. **Self-evaluation:** A great starting point is to ask each employee to judge his or her own current performance in key categories such as financial achievement, team development and personal improvement. I have found that most people are much tougher on themselves than a manager would be. Taking that into account, this is a helpful baseline for building a formal evaluation.
4. **Regularity:** Rather than saving everything for one sit-down meeting each year, check in with your people during regular mini reviews. The key to making the annual performance review process run smoothly is staging informal reviews all year long. That way you can stay current and head off issues as they come up, which will circumvent most un-pleasantries during the formal review.
5. **Written evaluation:** Put your thoughts down in writing, let them marinate for a day or so and then review them again. When you feel confident about your written survey,

review it with your superior. You can also ask for input from an HR professional in your organization. Gaining fresh perspective from others may help you achieve greater clarity and objectivity.
6. **Open dialogue:** Conduct your evaluation discussions early in the day while everyone is fresh. Ask questions, encourage constructive dialog and be sure to focus much of the discussion on future achievements. The past is the past. You don't have to avoid it altogether, but you will achieve more by focusing on the future.
7. **Just the facts:** Generalizing about vague topics is a quick path to disagreement. Stick to measurable performance facts. Come to a review prepared with specific examples of any issues you want to cover. Don't gloss over the tough stuff; address it head on. If you postpone, the conversation will just become more difficult down the line.

Have my tips helped reduce your performance review anxiety? I hope so. It's always easier said than done, so keep practicing.

Choose your business books carefully
NBJ October 2019

I read few if any serious books during my first 15 years in business. Occasionally, I did scan newspapers and trade journals. But it was not what you would describe as someone who is reading to learn. Then one day a young man who worked in our accounting department popped into my office touting a Wall Street Journal book review of "In Search of Excellence." I thanked him, skimmed the review and gave it to my wife as a gift suggestion.

On Father's Day the book arrived. Graciously I picked it up and read a few pages and then a few more and then I couldn't put it down. This was my first serious book reading in a long time. In it, authors Tom Peters and Bob Waterman, who had studied top-performing American companies, shared some fascinating common success factors. Wow. There was so much to learn. More importantly, it could easily be applied to our little business. The experience changed my attitude about reading books and began an educational reading regimen that continues to this day.

For me, the magic of this business book was in the studies, examples and lessons. Together they made for a relevant, interesting, educational and *applicable* read. Suddenly, I was learning from reading—and becoming a more effective executive as a result. It made me want to keep digging. I knew that becoming more informed would pay off: I would be able to give better direction and make smarter decisions. And I did.

Tips for a starting a reading regimen: Here's how to build a quality reading routine for self-development. First, select books that are both interesting to you personally and relevant to your career growth.

Second, figure out which skills you most need to develop and find the books that will give you the most knowledge to improve those skills. For me, selecting the right people for my team would always be one of my most important decisions as a leader. So, I started sourcing books about recruiting and interviewing. I have read my share. And my all-time favorite is "Who" by Geoff Smart, which I recommended in a previous column.

Third, round out your reading with books about becoming a great leader. Two top reads on management and leadership are "Good to Great" by Jim Collins and "The Best at What Matters Most" by Joe Calloway. Patrick Lencioni and Marshall Goldsmith are also excellent authors on the subject of leadership.

Fourth, biographies of people you admire can be great learning sources, too. Just think about the leadership challenges of men like Lincoln, Churchill and Eisenhower. In particular, look for biographies of leaders in your profession. In my world of retailing, the biographies of Walmart's Sam Walton and Bernie Marcus, founder of Home Depot, have been inspiring and educational.

A few more thoughts:

- **Learn from your reading:** If you are not growing from the experience, you are reading the wrong material.
- **Apply your knowledge:** Quoting books to others only serves to make you look smart on the surface. It's what you do with your newly acquired knowledge and personal skills that really matters.
- **Start (and maybe end) with book No. 1:** A word of caution: The second book by a big author is rarely as effective as the first. So, always go for the debut release from a variety of authors.
- **Share your favorite books:** You can visit my website, joescarlett.com, for more than 60 reviews on books about business, leadership, history, biographies, education, politics and retailing.

Finally, pause and ask yourself this: "What is your learning agenda?" Ponder that for minute and see if you have a solid answer.

Common sense and effective leadership go hand in hand
NBJ June 2013

Leadership is not complicated. First, we need to work smart, and then we can go on to working hard. Working smart begins with a liberal application of common sense, so let's look at a few basic practices of people who lead effectively:

Set direction: Everyone wants to know where the ship is headed, so don't keep it a secret. Explain as much as you can and more often than you think necessary. Repetition is important. Experts say people remember only a small portion of what they hear, so repeating the message is essential to building a clear understanding your business-unit goals.

Support: Achievement takes place when people have the tools to get the job done. Your leadership role includes ensuring the right tools are close at hand and knocking down any obstacles that might get in way of productivity.

Engage: Everyone wants to be part of something, so engage your people as much as you can. When team members participate in the planning process, they will more clearly understand direction, plus they will be well positioned to make suggestions that could have a positive impact on the level of accomplishment.

Coach: The time you spend coaching and teaching pays off by multiplying productivity and reducing big, costly errors. You also earn the respect of your people. Perhaps most importantly, when you look back on your career, the highlights will most likely be the people you coached along the way.

Reward: When you teach your dog to do something you reward that behavior with a treat. People react the same way, except the treat is a pat on the back. It only takes a few seconds to acknowledge someone, so if you want more productive people, recognize those who achieve. Remember, recognition is still the No. 1 motivator.

Set the example: Model the behavior you expect from your team. If you want frugality, demonstrate it in all you do. If you expect team members to respect each other, go out of your way to show respect to every individual.

As you develop your leadership skills, let common sense be your guide. And that includes never letting your leadership position go to your head. Inflated egos have brought down more leaders than any other shortcoming. Be a common-sense leader.

Joe Scarlett, joe@joescarlett.com
Retired Chairman of Tractor Supply Company

10. STRATEGY

Executive advice: outfoxing the competition
NBJ August 2016

 Staying ahead of the competition is a full-time job for most everyone in business. Leaders continually check rivals' new products, technologies, processes, marketing and a whole lot more. There are many different methods for learning about the competition: observation, reading, site visits, professional associations, trade shows and personnel interviews.

 In the retail world it is common to spend time analyzing item selection and pricing in print advertisements from other companies. This may have some value, but it's really more of an exercise of looking in the rearview mirror. I call this followership. Staying current on your competitors' developments is important, but if that is all you do to keep your business current you are really following—not leading.

 To be truly creative and innovative in offering new and improved products and services you must not just watch what others are doing, but engage proactively on the ground level by "getting inside the minds" of your customer. It's essential to understand the culture of your customers and their current unmet demands. But it's even more important to anticipate their future needs. A few other thoughts about staying ahead:

> **A culture of innovation** is a key building block to winning the competitive race. Your culture should scream, "We can change and improve everything, and we can get it done yesterday!"

When outsiders describe your culture with the phrase "never satisfied," you are on the right path.

Brainstorming can lead to real breakthroughs. Gather your mavericks, challenge them, get lost and watch them put forth real innovative ideas. Inspire them to think like customers, as customers will be in the future. Many of their bright ideas won't work but some will, and there might just be a true breakthrough in the mix.

Listening to customers with a passion is essential to clear understanding of both their current and future needs. Employees who have the most customer contact can yield great information for the company. At Tractor Supply we listen in a variety of ways: regular store visits, internal advisory boards, occasional customer focus groups, and even visits with customers at their home or property.

Test, test, test every possible new idea. If you have a 10 percent success rate on new ideas and you test 10 ideas, you have one success—just one. But if you test 100 new ideas at a 10 percent success rate you achieve 10 successes. The math is simple: The more you test the more success you achieve, and the more successes you have the further ahead of your competitor you will be.

Celebrate ideas and improvements at every possible opportunity. If you reward a great breakthrough to further support a culture of innovation you will see more breakthroughs. The more credit your organization places on fresh ideas that really work the more fresh ideas you will find in your pipeline.

The formula for outfoxing the competition is simple: Primary focus on your competition = **follower**. Primary on your customer = **leader**.

Listen to your customer, not your competitor
NBJ February 2016

In the early 1980s when our Tractor Supply management team first began to gel, we found better ways to listen to our customer. First and most obvious was spending more time in stores observing, asking questions and listening carefully to everything we heard. Salespeople and store managers know the most about the customer, so we made it our job to listen and then act on what we learned from them.

One big issue we learned about by listening more was out-of-stock products, which we attacked at the outset. Subtler still was that most of our customers did not appear to be traditional farmers but a majority drove pick-up trucks.

We examined sales data and found that products relating to production agriculture were almost all in a decline, while pet and animal products, riding mowers, hardware and work clothing were all in growth mode. It took a while but based on open and honest listening, observing and studying we came to the conclusion that our customer had evolved from a full-time farmer to a hobby farmer. That conclusion dramatically changed the direction of the company. But that was just the beginning of listening to customers.

Advisory boards became another listening mechanism that provided amazing results. Tractor Supply store managers interact with customers regularly and have an authentic sense of the business. We began by inviting a dozen managers from all over the country to spend a few days with us analyzing the business. Once we said that we are "taking notes but not taking names" the fireworks began. One great idea after another about products, customers, operations and distribution flowed at an exciting, breakneck pace. Expanding further, we began holding vendor conferences to discuss our business relationships, and out of that flowed myriad new product ideas and hundreds of customer insights.

We also watched what our competitors were doing but did not rely on it solely for customer research. Our conclusion was that if you spend a large amount of time studying retail competition you are liable to become a follower. Listening primarily to the core customer helps you to become leader, not a follower.

There is another kind of listening opportunity called the customer "complaint," which should be considered an opportunity. In fact, a complaint that's taken care of professionally can actually build brand loyalty. A quick and positive response including a big "thank you" usually works best. At Tractor Supply, salespeople are empowered to listen and do "whatever it takes" to help customers with issues.

There are many different ways to listen to customers. Start by taking stock of your organization to see if your team is doing all it can to listen. The better you perform this skill, the better the ideas you'll have to power future growth.

Let's get along: courting the competition
NBJ June 2014

Business people often view competitors as the enemy. That means leaders have little or no contact with other leaders. Let's turn that tradition on its head: Why not communicate with others in the same business? There's little to be lost—and so much you can gain.

While certain competitive secrets must stay under wraps, there is a goldmine of noncompetitive communication that can lead to operational improvements, industry best practices and personal growth. For example, our retail trade organization shared non-competitive information including loss prevention, logistics and training that ultimately benefited us all. You might uncover mutual government regulatory challenges where collaboration helps both parties. You might learn about helpful resources and career-boosting contacts more quickly.

When I was on the road visiting Tractor Supply stores, I often called a leader of a farm store competitor for lunch and maybe a store walk-through or two. Regularly I received a warm response, which over time developed into many solid friendships, some of which exist to this day. We never gave away competitive strategic plans, but we did share plenty of mutually beneficial ideas. We frequently found that we had similar challenges in developing people, managing inventory and dealing with certain problem suppliers. By sharing suggestions and solutions about non-competitive issues, we both won.

While occasionally I got the old "heave ho" on a "prospecting" trip to a competitor's store, a majority of times store managers were more than gracious—and proud to talk about their stores. On these trips I could quickly glean things like product assortment, level of customer service and even small nuggets of wisdom about retail improvements that I could apply at Tractor Supply.

So rather than keeping secrets, start taking the initiative. Test the waters by inviting a peer from a competitor for coffee or lunch. You just might gain new knowledge—and possibly a new friendship. Make the first move. You have nothing to lose.

Learn from the best—your competition
NBJ August 2019

Technology is pushing our world forward at an accelerated pace. Things are changing rapidly. So, to stay out ahead of the curve in the business environment, leaders must be open and committed to learning constantly—often through the competition.

In my days in retailing, I obsessed about this. I didn't want to become the dinosaur. So, I developed a passion for learning all I could about the best of the best in our industry. Additionally, I began to investigate other industries. This appetite for uncovering new opportunities that could positively impact our company became a touchstone of my time at Tractor Supply.

Continuous education is an essential component of business success. It doesn't matter how you get there. Find your own way to a path of lifelong learning: It could impact your career in more ways than you realize. Here's how to get started.

Study online: Learn from your most successful competitors. Start by visiting their websites and researching other information online. If your admired competitor is a public company, there is almost no limit to the data you can gather on the internet. As you study and identify topics of interest, focus your efforts on organizations that appear to have the most innovative products, processes and people.

Make contact: If you know someone at a competing organization, try to arrange an occasional coffee or lunch. It's amazing what you can glean through casual conversation. You might even learn some interesting facts by asking about the company culture. And if you don't know someone, try cold calling the logical contact to start networking. Cold calling takes a bit of initiative, but it's surprising how often these situations work out well for both parties.

Talk to customers: To learn more about the products from some of your most well-regarded competitors, find ways to identify and talk with their customers. Then be prepared to ask insightful questions about those products, including quality, effectiveness and value. You can even investigate future products not yet on the market by connecting with salespeople and viewing sales presentations.

Take a tour: In many industries on-site visits can be enlightening. Call ahead and ask the competition about a tour. Many companies are proud to show off their businesses. In some cases, for example at restaurants, hotels and retail locations, you can simply drop in and ask for a tour. In my career I found that most retailers are eager to show off their stores, both showrooms and backrooms.

Network regularly: Attend professional events, trade shows and any other gathering where you could meet and learn from other professionals. Find the right people to talk with and then casually ask the right questions. And just keep going. Once and a while you will hit on a nugget of information that will be of significant personal and/or professional benefit.

Read more books: This can take time but often yields tremendous knowledge. Choose business books that will be of most benefit to what you do on daily, and ask others for recommendations.

Biographies about leaders in your industry can offer some refreshing inspiration, too. If you are in a rapidly changing field new books are released frequently, so keep a running book list on your phone.

Business is moving at warp speed. In this environment, the winners will be the ones who stay ahead of the curve by learning and innovating faster than the competition. The pioneering ideas at our company came from studying the industry, networking among competitors and visiting every place we thought could help us learn more.

Leaders: take the initiative to get things done
NBJ July 2017

Growing up most of us heard these words of advice: "Take some initiative!" In the professional world, those more experienced than us may have shared similar wisdom: "There are those who watch things happen and there are those who make things happen."

Get the universal message here? Action. Resourcefulness. Ingenuity. Make no mistake about it: Leaders need to take the initiative to get things done.

Part of taking the lead is not shying away from new ideas, which can make the difference between triumph and failure. The most successful leaders know how to speak out on fresh topics and trends that can inspire innovation and improvement. Strong leaders are not afraid to fail, either. They simply take the initiative to "test" a new idea and report back on what they learned, whether good or bad. Thomas Edison tested thousands of versions of his new light bulb before he found the one that really worked.

I have always encouraged my team to take the initiative to experiment with all kinds of new ideas. In retail, where I spent my career, testing new products is easy: Put a new sample product in a few stores. If it sells add it to more stores; if it fails mark it down, sell it out and move on. The more frequently you take the initiative, the more likely you will find success.

Initiative can take many different forms: Beyond product testing, people in top roles at companies must be willing to lead, rather than follow, in all aspects of business. One memorable example of this happened just after Tractor Supply went public in the 1990s. Rumors began to circulate that Walmart was going to enter the farm-store business. First there was chatter about one pilot store, but then the rumor grew to hundreds of stores. Needless to say, this rattled our leadership team, stockholders and many of our suppliers.

We could have hunkered down, rolled back our big plans and prepared for the onslaught from the big kahuna. Instead, we did the opposite. A key partner and I decided to take the initiative to find out what Walmart really had planned.

I called Walmart CEO David Glass, and to my great surprise he answered his own phone and knew who I was. We talked for a few minutes before he invited us to Bentonville, Arkansas. Less than a week later we walked into the Walmart home office.

We spent about an hour with Mr. Glass discussing a wide range of retail topics and were impressed with his knowledge of our little niche business. He told us that Walmart would open one farm store experiment with the goal of identifying a few high-volume products that could be added to Sam's Club stores.

One year later we bought the remnants of Walmart's one and only "County Farms" store. Mr. Glass kept his word, and I don't think they ever found those magic products for Sam's Club. With that behind us we could say with great pride that we took Walmart out of the farm store business.

Our proactive approach and the honest conversation with Mr. Glass gave us enough information and confidence to allay the fears of so many of our people. It gave us all we needed to push forward with growing our stores and continuing to develop our leadership teams.

Everyone has opportunities to be bold in business. Wherever you are in your leadership career, don't stick your head in the sand. Instead, stick your neck out and take the initiative that can propel your career forward.

A customer's complaint is a company's opportunity
NBJ October 2016

Sometimes just changing your perspective on customer service can change everything. Leaders can turn a perceived negative into an instant opportunity simply by flipping a customer complaint into an occasion for improvement. This shift in mindset is also a great way to kick off universal process improvement at your company.

When a business regards a customer complaint as an annoyance, it looks something like this: You're put on perpetual hold while waiting for a "customer service" agent on the phone. Maybe you write a well-thought-out letter or email and receive no return communication. Or in a face-to-face interaction about an issue with a product or service you're belittled or put off with plenty of excuses.

On the flipside, hotels have become a shining example of how changing your approach to customer service from annoyance to opportunity can directly impact business for the better. Multiple studies have shown that when a hotel responds quickly and professionally to a customer complaint, and then resolves the issue in a way that results in a positive outcome, the customer will actually become *more* loyal than if the issue had never occurred in the first place. What an opportunity: Do the right thing for a troubled guest and build stronger loyalty in the process. What business could ignore that?

The key to initiating this new behavior is empowering your customer service people to immediately turn what could be an unwanted distraction into the exact opposite—A second chance to repair a problem that could build business down the line through a lasting bond with the customer.

Here are some examples of how we have approached this very issue at Tractor Supply, which can be applied to many retail businesses:

- ➢ **Whatever it takes:** At Tractor Supply, we teach our team members to respond to a customer complaint with, "I will do whatever it takes to make it right for you." Those words

immediately disarm an upset customer, which paves the way for a swift and usually friendly resolution.
- **Happy home visits:** Occasionally a Tractor Supply customer has a problem with a piece of equipment on his or her property. It's not unusual for one of our team members to visit the customer and make the repair during a home visit. This simple but effective step can facilitate a deeper relationship with that customer, and often results in a great PR opportunity when the story is passed around the community.
- **Learn on the return:** Any returned product can be an expensive transaction. If the product is truly defective, we can turn the matter into a learning opportunity for both the store and the manufacturer. An immediate, proactive resolution can prevent future reoccurrences.
- **It's always personal:** Every customer interaction is an opportunity to learn someone's name. There is no substitute for addressing a customer by his or her first name. You are automatically building a deeper connection—and possibly a customer for life.

Any time you can communicate face to face with a person about your product or service, you have a special opportunity to sell future business and develop a line of trust. The ultimate goal? For your customer to say, "I like you, I respect you and I trust your product/service, so I will be back next time."

So, remember, even a largely unhappy customer can be giant opportunity. You just need to look at the situation from a fresh perspective.

Lessons from the retail floor: get close to your customer
NBJ October 2014

There's a talk I used to give about customer service. I gave it so frequently to store managers and sales people that many of my associates could practically deliver it verbatim. While my focus was on retail store transactions, the principles I taught apply to every business. Here are four keys to getting close to and, more important, keeping your customer.

1. **Learn a customer name a week:** In a retail store, addressing your customer by name creates a powerful bond that is hard for a competitor to duplicate. Think about your own experiences and recall how you felt the last time a salesperson addressed you by name. This principle applies to every business—greet by name and make your customer comfortable with you and the surroundings.
2. **Ask, "What are you looking for?"** Our goal was to engage in a meaningful conversation about the customer's needs. Ask the right—and right amount—of questions; dig deep so you clearly grasp the challenge at hand. The more you can probe about the real needs, the more likely you will identify the best possible product for the customer. The process may be different in your workplace, but the principle pertains to every business.
3. **Walk 'em to the product:** After ascertaining the real needs, take the customer right to the product. In many cases the product needs a complete explanation and requires a practical demonstration. The goal is for the customer to be able to use the product to fulfill the need, which is the simple completion of the sales process. The last thing you want is for the customer to return not being able to use the product for any reason.
4. **Practice "3's a crowd:"** When there are three or more people in line it's time to call for help and open the next checkout. When it is time to complete the financial transaction, don't hassle the customer with a long wait. In any business, the final transaction should be quick and pleasant. Don't ever give a customer a reason for a mind change.

Let's recap four core customer service principles: Know your customers by name, ask the right questions, show and explain everything, and close the sale quickly and amiably.

Complete the sale
NBJ June 2015

There are four key selling points that we continually hammered home at Tractor Supply sales meetings. They are aimed at the retail selling process, but these principles apply to just about any selling situation:

1. **Learn a customer name a week:** There is no more powerful selling tool than addressing a customer by name, and particularly by the name the customer prefers. It's not uncommon to walk into a Tractor Supply store and hear the cashier say, "Good morning, Charlie," or "Good afternoon, Mrs. Jones." Even as the person moves further into the store you will likely hear a sales person take a similar direct approach. The best starting point of any sales transaction is a friendly, personal greeting.
2. **Walk the customer to the product:** When a customer is looking for something, take him or her to the right area first. All too often retail sales people just raise an arm and point to some distant aisle. An old friend in the retail business taught me how to discourage "finger pointing" among employees. Our joke was to tell people that if we saw them pointing, we would bite their fingers off. Of course, I never actually bit anyone's finger, but you can bet that image was memorable enough to prevent most pointing. In any business it is just good policy to lead customers to products and educate them in as much detail as necessary.
3. **Ask the right questions:** The generic "Can I help you?" almost universally gets the common "No thanks, I'm just looking" response. We found that by simply modifying

the question to "What are you looking for?" we almost always elicited a clear response about a specific product or problem, which led directly to a productive sales conversation. Asking the right questions can start beneficial discussions—and, ideally, a final sale.

4. **Practice "three's a crowd:"** In retail terms this means if there are three people at the checkout, open the next terminal immediately. In a store, money collection closes the sale. Customers need to be checked out quickly and courteously so they leave with a good impression of the final process. No matter what your closing process, end on a positive note and you'll leave the door open for future transactions.

In one way or another we are all selling a product, process, idea or ourselves. Take another look at the four points above and ask yourself if you are doing all you can to be a sales success in life.

Enlist workers to help cut costs
February 2009

Challenging economic times require tough and different leadership skills. In any business the first concern has to be financial—make sure your business generates enough cash to both survive in the short term and be ready to take advantage of the upturn when it comes. In times like this, the less well-run competitors will struggle and collapse. Cash management has to be concern #1—remember, if your business runs out of cash, your business is finished.

Here are a few rules for survival:

1. **Engage your people:** Be more visible than ever, be honest and share the facts with your team. Employees are easily your number one asset in tough times. They want to stay employed. They will do whatever it takes, and will often be the source of new ideas to run your business even more

efficiently. Your challenge as a leader is to listen to your people more than ever before.

2. **Be more frugal than ever:** Share the expense numbers with your people and ask for their input and support in expense control, both in their part of the business and elsewhere in the organization. When you ask the right questions, and listen carefully, it is amazing how many good ideas emanate from the people who are actually doing the work. Again, your employees will likely be your number one source for expense control ideas.

3. **Cut most capital expenditures:** This is not a good time to be initiating large cash commitments to future growth unless you are very solid financially. This can be an opportune time to reopen previous capital and long-term financial obligations to renegotiation. Your business partners are interested in your long-term survival and, during tough times like these, can often be persuaded to change the terms of your obligations.

4. **Be a tightfisted inventory manager:** Take a tougher approach than ever to inventory. Don't buy it until you absolutely need it, and be sure to return all the excess. You would be surprised how many suppliers, if you just ask, will simply take it back in order to maintain your business. This is also a good time to renegotiate payment terms—ask for an extra 30 or 60 days. Extended payment terms can make a big positive difference in your cash position.

5. **Stay close to your customers and your suppliers:** Be more aware than ever of the financial health of your business partners. There will undoubtedly be a lot of business failures and you need to be able to anticipate those in order to protect your company. Bankrupt customers don't pay and bankrupt suppliers don't ship. Your key suppliers and customers should be willing to share their financial statements with you. Diligent study, regular communication and a good dose of "show me the facts" should prevent bad situations from turning into catastrophe.

Don't be an ostrich! Uncertain times can open all sorts of opportunities for your business. A few thoughts:

1. **Strengthen your team:** The available talent pool is growing rapidly. Now is the time to weed out the weak links on your team and add available, high-quality talent. A word of caution. If you significantly underpay, your new employee will leave as soon as the economy begins to turns around. Even though they are "available", pay them what they are worth, if you want them to be long-term contributors
2. **Innovate:** While your competitors are hiding in their foxholes, you can bring to market new products and services which can provide the momentum for your company to recover from difficult times faster than your rivals. If you manage your cash well, you can get a big jump on competition by innovating while the others are hibernating.
3. **Acquire:** Poor economic times always produce big opportunities to acquire other businesses, products, trademarks, real estate, etc. Stay plugged in and be ready to jump, because you never know where the opportunities will show up. Again, aggressively managing your cash position can prepare you to be opportunistic.

Tough times present different and very difficult challenges. Many businesses will fail, many will just survive and others will both prosper and prepare for the future. The great business leaders look at tough economic times and see "opportunity" everywhere.

11. TEAMWORK

You succeed when your team succeeds
NBJ May 2022

You can think of success as an equation: The success of individual team members adds up to the sum total productivity in your work group. Simply, when they are successful, you are successful. That means it's always in your best interest to help your people do the best possible job for the greater good. Here are a few pathways to success:

Support skill building: Self-improvement is human nature. Most of us are driven to consistently build and refine our skills. But as leaders in an organization, it's our responsibility to make sure people have the skills *to do the job*. That means constantly evaluating the best internal or third-party training processes and ensuring that coaching or mentoring happens at every turn.

Once basic operational skills are in place, forward-looking leaders will turn to skill building—developing talent who can move to higher levels of responsibility. In the long run, leaders earn respect and loyalty for their relentless efforts to build skills of the whole team.

Procure the right resources: It is hard to produce a finished product when parts are missing, the computer is down or instructions are unclear. I experienced this kind of frustration early in my career while managing busy checkout lines at a grocery store.

Our biggest service slowdowns—and frustrated customers—came when one of three things went missing: paper bags, receipt tape or change. You can guess what topics quickly made it to the top of my daily checklist.

As a leader, it's your job to make sure your team can do their job. Achieving planned results will only work if everyone has easy access to the right tools, supplies and resources for the production process to move smoothly.

Coach for success: Stay close to your team. Good leaders will spend a disproportionate amount of time coaching but also listening their people. Be available when your people want to talk and make them comfortable speaking to the boss. The hardest part? Really listening, which can be difficult for hard-charging leaders.

You will learn more from your team than anywhere else. I'm a believer that "those closest to the work know the most about it." Being in the daily mix will help you better understand the work, personalities and even special talents that can benefit your organization.

This is also an excellent time to gather process-improvement ideas. When you can hear—and see—suggestions in the field you may be able to respond more proactively, constructively and graciously, whether the idea is adopted or not. Listening early can often identify problems when they are minor, allowing for quicker, less costly course correction.

One of the most powerful organizational cultures is "servant leadership," or providing the support that *every individual* needs to be successful. Leaders are always under pressure to complete tasks, but the most successful leaders can balance deliverables with duty—developing the talent of everyone on their team.

Lessons learned: fill your office with 'stars'
NBJ Feb 2012 (Original title: Surround Yourself with "Stars")

People are by far the single most valuable component of any business. Basic corporate strategy encourages perpetual upgrading of the team in order to build a stronger organization. That's why companies are in constant competition to recruit, develop and maintain the very best talent possible.

The problem is, exceptionally talented people—the stars—can be threatening, which can cause ripples in any growing company. When executives and managers are expected to hire and promote people who may in fact be smarter and better at the job at hand, corporate culture can get uncomfortable quickly.

There's good news: Following company protocol while still protecting your role and supporting your team is absolutely possible. It just takes a little perspective, because in reality stars lift everyone up. Here's how stars make the corporate world go round:

Self-reflection: Building a team of stars will almost certainly produce commendable results for your business unit. If you are ambitious and look into the future, you will probably realize that this kind of accomplishment makes *you* look good for hiring and leading the best team.

New opportunities: Putting together a team of stars that accomplishes outstanding things can open doors of opportunity for you personally. Top management views talent producers in a very positive light and will often consider this aspect of leadership when making decisions about promotion. As a talent builder, you will gain attention and respect—and perhaps additional responsibilities and advancement.

Less stress: Having great talent on your team can only help your group produce more and better results while ideally helping your unit function more efficiently. Highly capable stars might just make your work life easier by reducing stress and allowing you a little more time to focus on what you do best.

Everyone improves: Remember, improvement is the product of a great team. Really bright people will push and challenge you in ways that may at first make you feel uncomfortable. They will ask "why" when no one else does and they will raise questions about current and past practices. Embrace it—you are all moving forward and improving for the greater good.

Surrounding yourself with stars is a win-win proposition. If you want to get ahead, your team stars will lift you up. If you are happy where you are, you can help your stars get ahead and in turn gain respect for your talent-building skills. Enhancing the talent level of your own team will enhance the future of your entire organization.

Leaders work together, build trust
NBJ September 2020

Trust is the most basic building block of successful relationships. In a trusting environment you have a greater potential to overcome obstacles and achieve success. When a team and its leaders work together, openly depending on each other, there are no limits. The most respected leaders build organizations that are rooted in integrity.

In day-to-day operations you have to trust that if I say I'm going to do something that I will really do it. You have to feel confidence that I've told you the whole story and am not holding back. In order for us to work together effectively you have to trust me and I have to trust you. It is not complicated, in theory.

However, in practice trust must be based on shared values and built over time. Honesty is one of the values that has to shine through in all relationships. A lack of it, including making false promises, spreading rumors, plagiarizing, playing favorites or blaming others, can quickly sour any relationship.

That said, mistakes happen. And they can be fixed with transparency. Regardless of the reason, if you realize that you were not honest on a particular topic, your immediate goal should be to return to the original communication with an apology and a clarification. If you take action voluntarily and quickly enough the level of trust in your workplace relationship may not experience any setback.

Seeing trust in action: Leaders earn trust by modeling expected behavior. We all know that employees take behavioral cues from their leaders. So, for example, if respect is a key value at your company, it is incumbent on you to show respect to others. If you demonstrate disrespect, you will begin to lose the trust of your team. Good leaders model the right behavior at work and everywhere else in life. Said another way, leaders are always on stage.

Trust can erode quickly in times of great stress. Suppose you're late with a project: Everyone is working overtime and your boss is putting the hammer down. Sound familiar? During times like these tempers often flare and sometimes people say things that they later regret. We're human. The great thing about trust is it can often be rebuilt with a simple apology and a handshake. You'll never regret extending a heartfelt "I'm so sorry." And you may even get one in return.

Likewise, when big changes are taking place in your organization there is usually much uncertainty in the minds of your team. Leaders can alleviate such stress by communicating what they know, deliberately and in-depth. Then listen and respond to questions as best you can. It is also just fine to say, "I don't know, but I will try to find out." Times like this present much opportunity to build trust.

Recognizing good performance whenever and wherever you see it also builds trust. Celebrate positive outcomes. Reward breakthrough ideas. Make everyone on your team feel good about individual and join efforts.

Your conduct as a leader is everything. You build trust when you are honest, fair, open, authentic and caring. You earn trust when you show trust.

Tips for winners
NBJ June 30, 2017

It may be surprising to know that being a winner is not all that complicated. There are some very basic things everyone can learn and practice to become a winning leader. None of these "tips" require any special talent or advanced education—just some common sense and a commitment to being a good team player in the workplace. Try giving yourself a grade on each one, and then if you're really brave share your grade with someone close to you.

Be on time: It sounds easy, but for some people it's not. In most jobs, being on time is absolutely essential for the team to function. It shows respect for your boss and your peers. My philosophy is if you're on time you're late: My meetings start at five minutes before the hour.

Be prepared: Have the tools of your trade with you. That could be a hammer and nails or a charged computer. Be prepared with the skills you need to perform the job. Start work ready and able to be the best that you can be.

Work hard: Do what you're supposed to do when you're supposed to do it—with the diligence expected. Pull your weight so you don't disappoint other members of the team. Hard work is so important at Tractor Supply that our mission starts, "Work hard, have fun and make money."

Do the right thing: I believe that leading from an ethical position always puts you out front. Walk the high road in everything you do. Be safe, be thoughtful, and be honest in your words and actions.

Be positive: Smile, communicate and show everyone around you that you are an all-round good person. People want to work with other positive people—no one wants to be associated with a negative attitude. All the research shows that an upbeat attitude leads to a longer life, happier marriage and better career. Stay positive—it pays!

Be coachable: When you are open to learning, others will help you improve your skills and grow in your position. Leaders find that those who are most coachable are often the ones who are first to move up the ladder.

Be respectful: Be nice to other people, ask questions, hold the door, pat someone on the back, be polite—in other words do what your parents taught you for so many years. Demonstrating respect for others earns respect for you. Be nice—it works!

Be a team player: Go the extra mile to help your peers and team achieve success. Winners encourage and lead teams to work together toward a common goal. The extra effort will not only be observed by your boss, but also admired by your team.

As a leader, just think how great everything would be in your operation if everyone in your group followed each of these small pieces of advice every day. We can all be winners!

JOE SCARLETT

Work too hard?
Try measuring achievement
NBJ January 2010

Early in my career, one of my mentors took me to task about recognizing the difference between activity and accomplishment. I was often working hard and fast but simultaneously falling short of my goals. He coached me to stand back and evaluate my actual business achievements. My career took a swift positive turn once I made up my mind to measure myself by accomplishment, not activity.

It did not take me long to realize that being a good servant leader could do wonders for the productivity of my team. My focus shifted to assuring that my people had all the tools, processes and support to achieve maximum results.

Life as a leader got better as I became a better servant leader.

It is important for us to realize that it is not individual performance that produces optimum results. It is team accomplishment that is the overarching measure of success. Leaders should be focused on bottom line results (accomplishments), not how many hours we work or how hard we work. When your team is successful, you are successful.

Team productivity starts with the leader getting involved in planning, allocating resources, delegating, measuring, and rewarding, so get out from behind your desk and go where the action is. There is a mountain of truth in the old adage that "the people closest to the work know the most about it." If your people have clear direction, solid processes, and the right tools and equipment, they will most likely produce the results you are striving to achieve. If your people are frustrated by the lack of any of these, the productivity of your team will suffer. Your support is essential. When all is working well a few "pats on the back" can only add to the momentum you have built.

Good servant leaders are approachable. Good servant leaders are great listeners. When you hear criticism, the only response is "thank you." It is difficult to listen to criticism particularly when it is directed at your plans and initiatives but that criticism is the most important feedback you will receive. If you are defensive and argue with people's perceptions, or "shoot the messenger", you will likely shut off the feedback for good. A servant leader's role is to listen, support and knock down the obstacles so your people can perform.

Encouraging better ideas from your team is a winning recipe. Your people will perform more effectively and they will respect and admire you for your support and encouragement. The best executives are true servant leaders.

12. FAMILY

The key to juggling work and family
NBJ January 2016 (Originally "Balancing work and personal time")

These days only weird weather calls for more conversation than the hot topic of work-life balance. People are grappling with the constant tension between work and family time. Most professionals can achieve a reasonable balance but it takes discipline, planning and commitment—lots of it. With a new year upon us, there's no better time to start working toward more work-life balance.

Analyze the past year: Go back through your calendar to list and count key personal events like vacation time, long weekends, holiday events, family birthdays, celebrations, etc. Then go back and do the same analysis of work-related events—big meetings, conventions, annual industry events, company celebrations, etc. Now you have good history. Work through each item and note how you might want to handle things differently next year. Then review your notes and thoughts with your spouse or others close to you.

Build a plan: Get out next year's calendar and start by plugging in work events that you are required to attend. Then inquire with higher-ups about other events that might be planned or in the works so you get as clear a picture as possible. Add in birthdays. Discuss family vacations with your loved ones. What can you afford and where would everyone like to go? Do the research, build your plan and mark your calendar well in advance.

Share your plan: Spend quality time with your spouse and family talking about the plan and then adjust as it makes sense. If you have young children, set a reasonable goal of four family dinners a week and then keep track of your success. If you feel comfortable you can even share your plan with your boss, who then is more likely to be supportive throughout the year. Getting acknowledgement and "buy in" from those around will only help you achieve your plan.

Stick to your plan: Now comes the hard part—actually achieving your life-work balance goal. You might try holding yourself accountable by posting your plan where you can see it every day. You can also task family members or trusted co-workers with reminding you about keeping a balanced mix of time. If you have not been balanced in the past this will become a moderate to severe lifestyle change, which requires diligence and consistency. It's up to you to stay with your plan and only deviate in the most important circumstances.

I have found this life-balancing format to be effective throughout my career while working for a variety of bosses—some who did not care and some who did. I hope this formula works as well for you as it did for me.

Coaching our kids
Green Hills paper September 2013

Each day in our professional leadership roles we teach, push, encourage and reward. We rally our team members in effort to achieve maximum success. We are, in essence, coaches.

As parents, we are also coaches for our children. Just like with our team at work, we want each child to be wildly successful. We encourage them to follow their dreams because we want our youngsters to be happy in life. We also want to give them the freedom to choose their own career—one that they believe is the right fit for them.

The tough part is helping our children weigh risks and rewards. Do we want our kids to follow a dream that leads to no job or just a low-paying job? Probably not. I often hear parents and grandparents talk with mixed pride about a daughter who has a degree and is now making just above the minimum wage because that's what the particular field pays. Or worse, a son can't find any work in his chosen field and is now working in an industry that has no relation to the degree he worked so hard to earn.

Just as we coach for success at work, we need to give our children career coaching that will lead to solid professions. Quite frankly, it's a lot easier to be happy when you're making $75,000 a year than $35,000. We have a parental obligation to gently guide our children into careers that will be rewarding and satisfying both personally and financially.

Part of that coaching as a parent includes staying in tune with the times—knowing which jobs are in most relevant and in demand, and therefore profitable, in the current marketplace. Here are some examples of strong jobs today:

> Health care: dentists, nurses, pharmacists—almost anything in the field
> Technology: systems analyst, software developer—you name it in technology
> Engineering: civil, mechanical, electrical, etc.
> Professions: lawyers, accountants and managers

We love our kids and grandkids; so, let's use our coaching skills to position them for a lifetime of success.

Coaching youth about life, career
NBJ July 2016

One truly rewarding part of being a leader is handing down knowledge to the next generation. Coaching young people about life comes with the territory, but shaping someone's career often gives leaders as much inspiration as it does to those being mentored. Experience gives us the ability to listen, guide, direct and challenge the career thoughts of youngsters.

My philosophy has been to start with the big picture. I try to get young folks to develop a broader vision for where they want to go in life. But to be honest, I recognize that few teens have a clear plan for the future. However, I have also learned that for many youngsters it's preferable to talk to an "outsider" about careers rather than their parents, who often infuse the challenging topic with their own expectations and baggage.

Over many years of attending corporate conferences, mentoring workers, learning hard lessons in the business world and banking a variety of hands-on teaching experiences, I have collected some pointers for the next generation of professionals. Full disclosure: I borrowed part of a framework for success from an expert on youth development, but have added my own spin as my coaching formula has progressed.

Let's look at three key stages that can lead to great success in work—and life.

1. **Directing education:** The first critical step is to get the *right* education. Of course, any higher education will be helpful in the professional world, but an education tied to a focused career plan can be exceptionally powerful. Leaders can help teenagers narrow career interests by discussing natural skills, passions and curiosities. We can also facilitate learning by arranging some direct exposure to work environments—trying a part-time job, shadowing a specific worker, touring a workplace and meeting with other young people on the job. The goal is to help make the connection between a targeted education and career ambitions.

2. **Chasing a career:** The second step is actually finding and securing the job that's right for you, a topic on which most senior leaders can provide important assistance. The key message is explaining to job-seekers that finding the ideal position is a "full-time job" in itself. The process requires diligence, persistence and thick skin. Young people must be prepared for rejection, not sheltered from it. There will be a lot of "no's," but it only takes one "yes" to get a career moving.

3. **Securing support:** Third, our most important leadership decisions come down to choosing to surround ourselves with the right people—in business and life. With compe-

tent, caring, courageous people by your side, your odds of success are very high. Young people need to understand the importance of making good decisions about the people they choose to spend time with, and, when the time is right, a life partner who will be there to support them in whatever career direction they decide to go in.

When you are coaching young people about careers it's worth discussing these three simple points. The right education, job fit and support network is a solid blueprint for success.

Start planning your vacation now
NBJ November 2013 (Orig. "On vacation time")

When it comes to vacation, don't take a back seat. Now is the time to start planning your vacation schedule for *next* year. The sooner you begin the process the more successful you will be in obtaining a real break for yourself and your family, regardless of whether you have four weeks of vacation or one.

Communication: Start discussing vacation ideas and expectations for next year's travel. What does each family member or traveling companion want to do? Go to the beach, read a book and relax? Or explore lots of different destinations? These conversations can be particularly challenging when planning around small children or testy teenagers, but the sooner you start talking the sooner you can reach a compromise that will ensure everyone looks forward to vacation.

Research: Once some ideas are on the table, send away for brochures and gather some travel books about potential destinations. Planning is part of the fun. Get family members or traveling companions involved in discussions, asking everyone to read and make recommendations. Will your vacation include teaching your children about history and geography? If so, help them participate in the research.

Details: If you decide to spend a week or more in one location, consider how you'll allocate your time in that single area. If you want to lie on the beach, get some good reads lined up ahead of time. If you plan to take side trips, get your itineraries in order before you arrive. Making early reservations also gives you the best availability and sometimes the best prices. Plus, packing will be much easier if you start developing a list of items months before you're scheduled to leave.

Goals: This is one business tool worth applying to vacation. It's OK to set some personal or group goals about what you want to learn and agree on some specific attractions and historic locations your family wants to visit. Need or want to see some relatives or old friends en route? See if a short visit fits into your travel itinerary—without sabotaging precious down time.

The key to a great vacation is to plan early, talk through options, dig into the details and set some reasonable goals. Or just take my mother's wise advice: Take twice as much money and half the clothes you think you'll need. Happy travels!

It is never too late to plan your year
NBJ December 2017

How many times do we hear people exclaim, "I don't have enough time"? There's no time to accomplish this or that. I can't possibly squeeze that trip in now. How can I make both the conference and my kid's birthday? There's only one way to avoid falling into this trap: Plan ahead—way ahead. Long-term planning will ensure people with differing agendas don't sidetrack your life.

It's not as hard as it may sound. You've simply got to take charge of your calendar. Don't let other people or unforeseen events control your time. Yes, certain emergencies will crop up, but as counter-intuitive as it sounds, the more planned you are the better you will be able to deal with them. Block off key events in your calendar as early as you can—don't procrastinate. Also, learn when and how to simply say "no."

A commanding annual plan will help you achieve the results you value most, and you can start right now. Remember it's your life and your calendar, so take charge!

1. **Company functions:** You probably already know when big company events—sales meetings, strategic reviews and even the annual Christmas party—are scheduled. Check those key dates and put them in your calendar today so you don't accidentally double-book yourself.
2. **Industry functions:** Most leaders at organizations attend outside functions like trade shows, conferences and professional meetings. These are typically scheduled years in advance so that's a no-brainer: Book them in your calendar right now.
3. **Professional development:** We all should set aside meaningful time every year for our personal growth. Figure out what experiences you need to have and what topics you need to learn. Talk to your boss and maybe the HR department for counsel and support. Build a developmental plan and get it on the calendar before it falls through the cracks.
4. **Personal time:** Some of the most important dates and events lie outside of the professional realm, and it can cause undue stress on relationships when you forget a spouse's birthday, for example. So, book those personal dates, anniversaries and annual traditions before you have to ask for forgiveness.
5. **Family vacation:** Last-minute vacations are tough to pull off and can unnerve family members. Give yourself some well-deserved time off—and something everyone can look forward to—by arranging the family vacation now. Make it fun—gather everyone around the calendar and get to work carving out a week of true downtime—before other priorities take the place of family time.

Plan as far in advance as you can. Review professional events with your boss so that your plans are clear; then move on to your personal agenda by proposing ideas and talking to those closest to you. You won't complete your annual plans all at once, but the sooner you get started the sooner you can make decisions.

Of course, we all need to allow for a little leeway—it's life!—but starting with a solid plan will help you stay on target. Set a date to complete your plans for the year. Then sit back and enjoy the surprising freedom that comes with thoughtful planning.

For mental fitness, invest in yourself first
NBJ January 2021

Maybe you already invest in yourself by exercising several times a week, eating the right foods, maintaining a healthy weight, and seeing the doctor at least once a year. Everyone knows that physical fitness increases our ability to function in life, including performing as top-notch leaders.

But equally important in business is keeping our minds functioning for maximum achievement. Look around: I'll bet the high performers you know are people who are continually studying and learning. The better your command of how your business works, the more productive you will be. Just as being physically fit can yield great confidence, so does maintaining mental fitness.

Keep learning to stay on top: Ask yourself what skills you could improve on and then map out a plan to really step up those skills. Consider all your options—taking key classes, reading targeted books and trade magazines, networking, practicing public speaking and attending industry events.

Ask a superior for advice: Let your boss know that you want to improve your skills in effort to produce even better results. Ask for an honest evaluation and ideas about skill development. Ask for a meeting and follow up on your request. I remember when my boss made two suggestions about classes that I did not think made sense at the time, but in the long run both were very important in my growth. In most cases you will wind up with more good ideas than you can handle.

Find a mentor: You might get even more value from finding a mentor who can guide, coach and challenge you. I was fortunate to have two significant mentors in my life: my father, who regularly associated with business leaders and shared so many stories that helped me develop a good grasp of business leadership, and my Tractor Supply Company predecessor, Tom Hennesy, who challenged my skills and helped me continually mature into a solid leader.

Involve your family: Your family should also be part of your self-investment plan. After all, they know you best. Case in point: Some of the soundest advice of my life—the kind I don't always want to hear—comes from my wife. So, communicate with those closest to you, take all tips in stride, and say thank you, because it may be some of the best counsel you ever get.

Minimize stressors: You can't avoid all job-related stress but you can minimize it with practices like continuous education and delegation. The more you educate yourself about operations in your area, other parts of your organization and the people in your work world, the more you'll experience a sense of global control over your day-to-day tasks. You can further minimize your stress by training and coaching your team so you can confidently delegate key tasks without having to over worry about follow-through.

Pass it on: There's no better feeling than passing on what you've learned—and that can directly impact your emotional health. I was fortunate enough to return favors I've received over the years by mentoring a young man in Nashville. For years we had breakfast conversations about both personal and business development. Today his business is more than 10 times the size it was when we first worked together, and I feel honored to have helped in some way.

So, remember, invest in your whole self. Look in the mirror and assess physical and mental fitness. Build a plan. Engage those around you. Commit to continuous growth in every aspect of your life. Remember, no one's going to take a risk on you if you don't invest in yourself first.

13. SCARLETT OP-EDS

The metrics of good business
NBJ—January 25, 2013

Around the globe, temperature is measured in Celsius, weight in kilos and liquids in liters. The rest of the world is on the metric system. Why aren't we?

Every time I travel outside the country it becomes obvious that the United States is hurting itself by hanging on to an antiquated measuring system. International trade is essential to our economy yet nearly every transaction requires various conversions from our imperial measuring system to metric units. We are simply not communicating in the same basic numeric language as the rest of the world.

World leader to follower: Sadly, we missed our initial opportunity. The United States Mint, formed in 1792, produced the world's first decimal currency. For more than two centuries our country led the world with the first metric-measured currency, yet we are likely to be the last to adopt metric for other measures.

In fact, the U.S. is one of only three countries including Liberia (Africa) and Burma (Asia) to still use the tricky imperial measuring system. We continue to struggle with eight ounces to a cup, two cups to a pint, four pints to a quart and four quarts to a gallon when we could easily measure in liters, using the decimal system for larger and smaller quantities.

A simpler system: The great thing about the metric system is it's simple and logical. And it's already all around us:

- The shipping or sale of almost anything in our country shows the metric measure in addition to our system.

- Most items in your pantry include imperial and metric measures on packaging.
- Wine and liquor are sold only in metric measure and no one is complaining.
- Our kids learn about metric in school but never get a chance to use it.

Imagine if all business could be conducted with the same units of measure? While it might take some time and effort, we can help move our country into the 21st century. Here are some ways you can encourage the move toward universal measurement—and smarter international trade:

- Talk about metric measure at every opportunity
- Challenge others on this topic whenever you can
- Write about the benefits of universal measurement
- Communicate with any politician you think might listen
- Share this article

Comments:

1. Couldn't agree more. Like so many things this is an example of how the most advanced, cutting-edge country in the world is also, when it comes to certain culturally-based anachronisms, also the most backward thinking... John Ratliff
2. Dear Joe, only when enough business people and engineers, scientists etc. speak up will this get this done. Mathematics teachers around the US have had to continue teaching both systems which in the modern era is a time-consuming deal when there are other more important topics to teach. You are so right in that the metric system is much easier to learn and apply and it fits in with our monetary situation. Since I retired in 1999 it is amazing that we have not done what you are proposing. We have discussed it since the late 70's. I am not sure what the powers to be use as their reason not

to do it. I think you and I have discussed this before and for some reason nothing has changed. What do you hear from your business leaders as to why? Jim Moyers
3. Yes, that would indeed make things a lot more efficient! I spend a decent bit of time in Ontario and our measuring system is one thing that never ceases to baffle the Canadians! Mike Lanzara

Let the free market live!
City paper August 15, 2010

Our free marketplace is not perfect—and never will be. But it is the most spectacular, wealth-generating machine in the history of the world.

No one likes what has happened to our economy recently, but we should never forget that wealth is created by individuals and business—not government. Our systems of economic freedom, innovation and entrepreneurship will continue to generate powerful, long-term growth—as long as we don't mess it up.

Paralysis of perfection: Our nation was founded on the principles of freedom that include limited government and maximum personal rights. We cherish our right to freely pursue any legal business opportunity with minimal government restriction. That's how our phenomenally successful system works.

More government regulation only means a higher cost to do business, which translates to consumers paying higher prices for goods and services. Attempting to regulate ourselves to perfection will only lead to paralysis.

Right now, we can still try any "wild and crazy" idea for a new product or service, as long as we don't violate the various laws and regulations. Often it is these very wild and crazy ideas that lead to innovation and wealth creation. These are ideas we should encourage and celebrate.

Incentive to innovate: Suppose you have an interesting idea about a new product. You borrow a little money, buy some raw materials, assemble your product and then sell it. Most ideas fail, but let's say yours works. Next you rent a building, lease some equipment, and hire an engineer, a few production folks, an accountant and a sales person. You are creating a product for customers, employing a half-dozen people and generating wealth that you will likely reinvest in your growing start-up business. This is the American way.

As this scenario demonstrates, wealth is created by individuals and businesses, not government. But government can redistribute wealth. It's a vicious cycle. The more we borrow to redistribute (to be paid back by future taxes), the more we increase taxes and impose additional regulations, which in turn discourage our entrepreneurial spirit. The more the government takes and regulates, the less incentive individuals have to innovate and produce.

Beware of "I'm here to help:" The unintended consequences of government oversight and regulation are often beyond comprehension. After the round of Enron scandals Congress passed the Sarbanes Oxley Act which was supposed to prevent all sorts of monkey business yet after just a few years we had the Madoff scandal and the big banking meltdown. And on top of that American business is now forced to spend billions annually in compliance costs which has made our country just a little bit less competitive in the global market. Government oversight inevitably slows and sometimes paralyzes the very businesses it is intending to help.

Our capitalist system makes big mistakes but also creates incredible wealth. The continual process of business failures and bankruptcies are key ingredients in the process because from the ruin's capital is redeployed where it can be more productive. In addition, failures are learning tools that help inspire new ideas and new businesses. The faster business changes the faster it grows.

The current march toward greater and greater government regulation is a march toward business mediocrity. The more complex the oversight the slower our great wealth generating machine operates. People come from everywhere to participate in our economy because they see greater opportunity here than in their own countries. Free people and free markets generate the ideas that have made our economy the envy of the world. Our politicians should be encouraging those free markets and minimizing business regulations and controls.

Our collective objective should be to support and encourage ethical and transparent wealth-creation business and industry. We do have the best economic system in the world, and no matter what has happened recently, we should never forget how we achieved such success in the first place. The free market is our wealth generator, and the wealthier the nation, the more opportunity for *every* citizen.

Government bailouts are a problem, not the solution
NOVEMBER 2008

In the old days bank robbers went to jail. Today, the bankers and the robbers are one and the same, and they are being rewarded for incompetence with huge bags of extra money, courtesy of us taxpayers.

We have centuries of history that prove that markets don't go up forever. Bankers, more than almost any other group, should know this and if they do not, they should not be bankers. When bankers give mortgages to those who obviously can't repay, there is a serious shortage of basic common sense (or maybe just plain stupidity) as well as a lack of financial responsibility to stockholders and customers.

When you look at today's banking and real estate crisis, it is clear to even the least sophisticated among us that common sense has been lacking and basic ethics are out the window. Congress has now committed $700 billion to the very people who got us into this mess—a massive obligation belonging not to the politicians but to current and future taxpayers. Too late—it is a done deal

Bankruptcy may help the Big 3: Congress is now focused on bailing out the Big Three automakers who we all know have been on a downward spiral since the '70s or maybe earlier. The idea that GM, Ford and Chrysler would all of a sudden get smart after decades of being stupid is naive. It is conceivable that they might wake up after going through Chapter 11 bankruptcy, so let's give them that opportunity.

Suppose we do bail out the auto industry, then, what is next? How about the boat and yacht business, which I understand is now close to a standstill? And the homebuilders represent a huge portion of the economy and they are all in big trouble.

The restaurant business has been doing poorly since the spring and we certainly would not like to see our favorite spot close down. And then we don't want to forget all the retailers that are on the ropes.

Our free-market capitalist economy is the envy of the world. There have been some excesses along the way, but our basic job-and wealth-creating machine is the best on the planet.

I have been in business all my life and never dreamt of any kind of government help. I figured that if we did the right things, worked hard and stayed in close touch with our customers, we would do well. And to the contrary, if we did not do well, we would fail. That's business—let's not monkey with our principles.

We are at the top of a slippery slope that is leading us in the direction of socialism. Bailouts are a sickness; let's not get any sicker.

Public option will be expensive, inefficient
NBJ November 2009

It sounds so simple to have Uncle Sam simply set up a medical insurance operation to assure fair competition. We have been told that there will be no taxpayer subsidy so it will simply be a matter of collecting premiums, paying benefits and covering overhead expenses.

Starting any business, and, make no mistake about it, this is a business, requires capital investment and, in this case, a massive one. So, your tax dollars will provide the "seed" money to get this operation off the ground.

You can count your initial investment in the billions. How many billions? We don't have any idea. Undoubtedly, the capital to start the business will be borrowed, which further adds to our growing national debt. In business, debt must be either paid back or serviced with interest payments which come from operating income. It is hard to believe that a federal insurance operation will either pay interest or repay the debt.

There are 1,300 companies providing medical insurance to Americans.

These companies compete with each other to profitably grow their businesses. There is certainly a lot of criticism directed at these companies about a variety of issues, but the idea that 1,300 companies with hundreds of thousands of employees could ever collude to avoid competition is simply unthinkable. Competition is the best and only real path to achieve efficiency in this or any industry.

Just look at Amtrak, which was taken over in the 1970s and is today gobbling-up billions of our tax dollars every year. Consider Amtrak's level of efficiency: For every dollar you spend on an Amtrak ticket, taxpayers send in another dollar. In business terms, their profit-and-loss statement reflects a 50 percent loss, which, in the free marketplace, is an express ticket to the bankruptcy court.

Government's job ought to be to set the rules, monitor the scoreboard and sit back to watch the competitive marketplace do the rest. Government ought to knock down regulations that impede competition. The idea that bureaucrats in Washington can achieve a greater degree of efficiency than 1,300 insurance companies is simply unrealistic.

Airline leaders are out of touch
August 2008

Those of us who are regular air travelers are just thrilled at all the new fees the big airlines are allowing us to pay these days. If you have traveled recently on the legacy airlines, you know that the management has worked overtime to find new ways to nickel and dime passengers. Checking a bag? Get your wallet ready—$15, $25, and if it it's over 50 pounds you may need to give them your first born. Hungry? Open your wallet but don't expect the food to taste as good as the pictures look. You want your sandwich warmed? Forget it. Want something to drink? I recently paid $2 for a glass of water. What will be the next new fee? Let your imagination work overtime on this one.

The traditional goal of the airlines is to provide professional, efficient and safe transportation from one location to another. Fee collection makes the process less efficient and less professional. Ticket counter personnel now have to collect luggage fees which pit the new process against an already tense customer. For the airlines this either costs more labor or forces us to wait longer at the counter. Flight attendants now have the additional and stressful task of collecting cash or credit most times a drink, snack or meal is served. These extra friction points are tough on airline employees as well as passengers.

If we were to apply airline style fee collection to the supermarket, we would have checkout counters in every department. Pay when you pick up the vegetables, pay when you select the meat, when you get your milk—you have the idea. So why are so many airlines moving to greater inefficiency? It makes no business sense.

Petroleum prices have gone through the roof and we all know that air travel is certainly going to cost more. When something costs more, charge more. Creating all these additional stress points and inefficiencies in air travel only exacerbates the whole air travel experience.

The one major exception to all this stupidity is "common sense" Southwest Airlines which consistently provides free soft drinks and peanuts for everyone. No new fees, no additional labor costs and no added stress for either employees or passengers. It is so simple: raise the ticket price so all the stress and all the collection occur at the purchase point which is usually separated from the travel day. It should also be noted that Southwest is by far the most (and often only) major profitable US airline.

One has to question the decisions made by airlines that put employees and passengers into additional confrontation points in a business already known for less than stellar customer relations. We often hear about the older airlines being in financial difficulty which leads to basic questions of leadership. If Southwest can do well in bad times as well as good times why can't the others. You have to wonder if the senior airline executives have ever worked the ticket counter, ever traveled as regular coach passenger and even whether they ever have talked to customers.

Congress should approve online sales tax rule
Knoxville News Sentinel November 2016

As the former chairman and chief executive officer of Tractor Supply Company, I'm often asked for guidance on running a successful business. My answer is always the same: You've got to do the right thing.

Tractor Supply is a values-driven company with zero tolerance for lack of ethics. The company works hard to do right by its customers, offering high-quality products and competitive pricing. We always followed the rules, paid our taxes and operated with integrity and honesty.

Doing business is never easy, especially in retail. I should know: I spent almost 45 years of my life working retail. And it's only gotten tougher in recent years, thanks to a loophole that lets out-of-state internet retailers avoid collecting and remitting state sales taxes.

In Tennessee, this means some internet retailers have nearly a 10 percent advantage over our local brick-and-mortar businesses. It's illogical and unfair. There's no justification for this bad policy.

Toward the end of my tenure with Tractor Supply in the early 2000s, we began to see the rise of the internet and its effect on local businesses. As people got more comfortable buying and selling online, we faced new competition from online retailers, and we worked harder to keep our customers happy.

However, no business can truly compete when playing against a stacked deck. And that's what this loophole is for internet retailers: a deck stacked in their favor.

Today, business owners have to deal with customers who come into their stores, spend time with the sales personnel, and then leave without buying anything because they'd rather get the same product online without paying the sales tax.

The federal government has tried to pass legislation that would finally fix this inequity, but Congress hasn't been able to get it done. By not addressing this issue, the government is effectively picking winners and losers in business—and that's wrong.

Fortunately, a growing number of states, including South Dakota, Alabama and several others, are considering their own policy changes to ensure all businesses play by the same rules—regardless of whether they're physically located in the state or operate online.

Now it's time for Tennessee to follow suit.

In the coming months, a Tennessee legislative committee will consider a new rule proposed by the Department of Revenue that would require all out-of-state, online-only businesses with more than $500,000 in annual Tennessee sales to collect and remit state sales tax. I join other local business leaders in expressing strong support for the approval of this rule.

This is about fairness, plain and simple. Tennessee businesses are creating jobs in our workforce, supporting local community initiatives and investing in the state economy. They shouldn't be held to a different standard than out-of-state internet retailers.

By supporting this rule, policymakers can promote fair competition across the board for all businesses. And, as an added benefit, the tax revenue that may be generated as a result presents an opportunity to explore additional tax reductions, helping make the rule revenue neutral.

In business, it's important to do the right thing. And now we need our elected officials to do the right thing for Tennessee business owners. I strongly urge our policymakers to approve the online sales tax rule and level the playing field, once and for all.

It's time to do the right thing and approve online sales tax rule
By Joe Scarlett

As the former Chairman and CEO of Tractor Supply Co, I'm often asked for guidance on running a successful business. My answer is always the same: you've got to do the right thing.

Tractor Supply is a values-driven company with zero tolerance for lack of ethics. The company works hard to do right by its customers, offering high-quality products and competitive pricing. We always followed the rules, paid the taxes, and operated with integrity and honesty.

Doing business is never easy, especially in retail. I should know: I spent almost 45 years of my life working retail. And it's only gotten tougher in recent years, thanks to a loophole that lets out-of-state Internet retailers avoid collecting and remitting state sales taxes.

In Tennessee, this means some Internet retailers have nearly a 10 percent advantage over our local brick-and-mortar businesses. It's illogical and unfair. There's no justification for this bad policy.

Toward the end of my tenure with Tractor Supply in the early 2000s, we began to see the rise of the Internet and its effect on local businesses. As people got more comfortable buying and selling online, we faced new competition from online retailers, and we worked harder to keep our customers happy.

But no business can truly compete when playing against a stacked deck. And that's what this loophole is for Internet retailers: a deck stacked in their favor.

Today, business owners have to deal with customers who come into their stores, spend time with the sales personnel, and then leave without buying anything because they'd rather get the same product online without paying the sales tax.

The federal government has tried to pass legislation that would finally fix this inequity, but Congress hasn't been able to get it done. By not addressing this issue, the government is effectively picking winners and losers in business—and that's wrong.

Fortunately, a growing number of states, including South Dakota, Nebraska, Georgia and several others, are considering their own policy changes to ensure all businesses play by the same rules—regardless of whether they're physically located in the state or operate online.

Now it's time for Tennessee to follow suit.

Later this year, the Tennessee General Assembly's Joint Committee on Government Operations will consider a new rule that would require all out-of-state, online-only businesses with more than $500,000 in annual Tennessee sales to collect and remit state sales tax. I join other local business leaders in expressing strong support for the approval of this rule.

This is about fairness, plain and simple. Tennessee businesses are creating jobs in our workforce, supporting local community initiatives, and investing in the state economy. They shouldn't be held to a different standard than out-of-state Internet retailers.

By supporting this rule, policymakers can promote fair competition across the board for all businesses. And, as an added benefit, the additional tax revenue that could be generated as a result should be dedicated to fund a different tax cut, such as a reduction on food sales taxes as some have suggested, ensuring the rule remains revenue neutral.

In business, it's important to do the right thing. And now we need our elected officials to do the right thing for Tennessee business owners. I strongly urge our policymakers to approve the online sales tax rule and level the playing field, once and for all.

Four-year college not for every Tennessean
Tennessean October 2014

Today not all career paths start at University Trailhead. While "follow your dreams" may sound like good advice, it does not provide enough concrete guidance for working in today's competitive marketplace. Instead of solely focusing on a college education, parents and teachers can provide kids and students the greatest service by opening up a conversation around different avenues that can lead to skilled and well-salaried jobs.

Four-year college is still the right choice for many. Two-year college or trade school may work best for students with other skill sets or narrowly focused interests. The key is to help the next generation focus on occupations that will lead to financial independence first, and then help them acquire matching education.

Beginning with the class of 2015, the Tennessee Promise is also helping this cause. It offers two years of tuition-free community or technical college to Tennessee high school graduates. Students will be paired with a partnering organization serving their home county and will be provided a mentor who will support them during the college application process.

By thinking outside the college box, we quickly see that plenty of respectable, good-paying jobs that don't require a four-year degree are going unfilled. For some, trade school and an apprenticeship or two years of focused training is all that's required before moving into the workforce full-time. Here are some of these work scenarios worth considering:

Welding together a solid future: Earlier this year I heard a radio ad in Jacksonville, Florida, that called for 900 welders to fill openings in the shipbuilding and repair business. Researching further this in-demand skill, I found that Middle Tennessee also has a shortage of welders. It's hard work, but very good pay.

Learning on the road: A recent *Wall Street Journal* article pinpointed a national shortage of more than 30,000 truck drivers. In fact, one Nashville company featured in the article said it has enough available freight for 100 more drivers but they can't find enough drivers to carry the cargo. Again, tough hours, but solid pay.

An auto mechanic occupation: In another recent article, automobile dealers said there is a nationwide shortfall of 90,000 auto mechanics. In our car-obsessed culture, you can bet there will continue to be plenty of mechanic openings in communities throughout the country. Another dirty job, but with quality compensation.

Building your way up: In our country there is a continual deficit of construction workers, a job that requires heavy manual labor—and not quite the paycheck it warrants. However, starting in construction can provide an opportunity to seek apprenticeships in other higher-paying trade positions such an electrician, plumber or carpenter. Starting at the bottom can get your boot in the door.

Not so hot and cold: Another steady trade that can garner a hefty paycheck is HVAC. A friend of mine in the heating and cooling business says that he is constantly looking for technicians who know how to install, maintain and repair equipment. Who knew keeping folks comfortable could be such a comfy career?

One maturing livelihood: With our massive aging population there is a near non-stop demand for healthcare professionals—nursing assistants, licensed practical nurses, dental assistants and technicians, and the list goes on. These are all well-paying jobs with almost unlimited options for the foreseeable future.

Life on—and above—the line: "Made in America" manufacturing is making a comeback. Just a few miles from here, in Chattanooga, Volkswagen will soon start adding 2,000 more employees to build a new seven-passenger SUV. All that's required? A two-year degree.

Count on computing: Computer technology currently represents the most occupational opportunities nationwide. Did you know there are 200,000 computer professionals from other countries working in the USA on H-1B visas because we don't develop enough competent technicians to cover our needs? Plus, we employ hundreds of thousands more remotely. Kids love technology. Opportunity abounds!

These are just a handful of examples of the prospects for quality jobs in Tennessee. Truckers, welders and nurses are largely a mature workforce, which means retirements will further increase demand. Likewise, there's a nearly never-ending search for qualified people in healthcare, technology and construction.

All these professions require getting focused—and getting educated. Let's encourage our young people to develop a vision for their futures—then use all our resources to get them on the right path to success.

Tennessee voices: charters must reflect high standards
Tennessean May 2014

During my nearly 30-year career as an executive with Tractor Supply Company, our business responded to opportunity and demand by adding hundreds of new retail stores across the country.

Because we had a quality product backed by an outstanding team, most of those stores became wildly successful and contributed to the overall strong performance of the company. But occasionally we had a store that did not perform and when we did, we simply closed it.

Any closure was both a disappointment and a learning experience. We studied the reasons for failure and learned how to avoid similar mistakes in the future. Based on that long term learning Tractor Supply seldom if ever closes a store today.

Businesses become stronger organizations through cycles of new idea experimentation which often led to success and often lead to failure. That is the process of strengthening. Today I see similarities in the experiences of successful business organizations and what is happening today in Nashville's public school system.

Nashville has a young but very successful charter school environment. An emphasis on quality leaders, teachers and schools is merging with increasing parental demand for school choice and the result is a large number of a high-performing public charters, and more are on the way.

Just like with my business, there have also been disappointments, as a handful of Davidson County charter schools, most recently Boys Prep, have been closed for failing to meet the performance standards in their contracts with Metro Nashville Public Schools.

Closure is an unfortunate circumstance for the parents who made decisions to send their children to those schools, but it is clearly the responsible thing to do. Schools chronically failing to meet the needs of their students should be closed. It allows parents and families to more expeditiously guide their children to a better school.

THE CULTURE WARRIOR

In Tennessee, MNPS and other local school districts grant charter schools autonomy to develop their own plans for academic programs, staffing and budgeting. In exchange, charter schools are held to appropriately demanding performance standards.

Those performance requirements are actually very well defined. Charter schools operate on a performance contract basis with local districts. When the schools do not measure up to the pledge in the contract, the district has the right to—and should—revoke the charter and close the school. The other trigger to closure is when a charter school lands in the bottom 5 percent of performance in the state.

I fully support MNPS's action to close underperforming charters—it is the right thing to do for parents, families and the health of the overall education system.

Strong accountability standards are a significant reason why Nashville's charter school movement is so successful. Yes, some schools have closed, but there can be no quarrel with the quality and performance of the vast majority of Nashville's charter schools.

Accountability for charters is good policy, so I will argue that MNPS should apply the same or similar accountability framework to district schools. The district's adoption of the Academic Performance Framework (APF) last year is a step in the right direction. The APF gives schools a composite rating on a host of key performance indicators and has started to force difficult conversations about chronically underperforming schools. Schools that receive the lowest rating on the APF for three consecutive years can face closure or turnaround by a charter operator.

The bottom line is that we cannot allow chronically underperforming public schools, be they traditional or charter, to continue to operate without consequence. A generation of students is counting on us to have the moral courage to demand excellence in public education.

JOE SCARLETT

Private industry can end prison recidivism

Wednesday, April 2021
Nashville Tennessean, Knoxville News Sentinel and Memphis Commercial Appeal

Your turn: Joe Scarlett Guest columnist. Way too many young people are in our jails, and a huge portion of them are repeat offenders. It is unfortunate that young people get into trouble and wind up in jail, but it is even worse when so many return to their detrimental ways and wind up back in prison.

We need to challenge ourselves to prepare inmates for successful reentry into society as fully employed, taxpaying citizens. A sensible investment on the front end would prepare inmates for success in the world and would be miniscule in comparison to the continuing cost of additional years of incarceration, which is approaching $30,000 a year to house a single inmate.

When private industry steps up: At a conference several years ago, I heard an inspiring story of long-term rehabilitation from an industrial-seating manufacturer in Kansas. After struggling to fill its skilled labor jobs, this company partnered with a local prison to set up a portion of its manufacturing inside the prison walls. The company hired prisoners as regular employees, taught them a valuable skill and, perhaps surprisingly, paid them competitive, market-based wages.

Think about that. An incarcerated individual, whose future presents little or no hope, learns a skill, masters basic work disciplines and puts real money in their pocket. Better still, at the time this story was told to me, many of these newly-trained individuals went to work in the factory after their release and none had returned to prison. When you have money in your pocket, you have confidence about your future. In some cases, these individuals left prison better off financially than they were at any other time in their lives.

Half of released prisoners quickly return to prison: Today, most of the incarcerated population leave prison with their personal belongings and a small amount of cash. It is not a stretch to assume that their destination is likely right back where they got in trouble in the first place, raising the odds that they could easily get back into the same old mess. According to a 2019 report by the Sycamore Institute, about half of the state prisoners Tennessee releases each year return to prison within three years.

Now compare these two situations—one person served their time and now has a set of marketable skills and a sense of self-worth. The other is directionless and could be on a pathway to return to incarceration. The long-term prospects for both are clear.

A societal challenge: The challenge for our society is to build skills, confidence, and character before release. This may look expensive—but the cost of recidivism is far greater, not only to taxpayers, but also to crime victims and communities as a whole.

The process of changing our ways must go first to government, to preach the importance of successful reentry and enacting better prison workforce and reentry programs. Fortunately, our state legislature is currently undertaking proposals by Gov. Bill Lee to remedy this problem.

Then, the challenge goes to prison operators to expand the proven work being done in pockets of prisons across the country into full-scale programs of skill and character building that can be accessed by all incarcerated individuals. Then, my friends in the business world need to open their hearts and wallets to support these initiatives and support these people who need our backing.

In my career, I took the most pride in the teaching and coaching I did to develop leaders in the company. This challenge is similar. We—all of us—can team up to make a life-changing impact on the futures of thousands of people. You will be so proud years from now when recidivism is reduced to nearly nothing by our collective efforts.

ABOUT THE AUTHOR

Joe Scarlett spent nearly thirty years in leadership roles with Tractor Supply Company, serving as both its President and Chairman. Since his retirement in 2007, Joe has dedicated himself to teaching and writing about leadership, and to improving educational outcomes for Tennessee students through the Scarlett Family Foundation. He resides in Nashville with his wife of fifty plus years, Dorothy.

Printed in the USA
CPSIA information can be obtained
at www.ICGtesting.com
LVHW091245021223
765394LV00047B/727